Pr

APPEAL TO THE COURTROOM

Powerful. Riveting. Poignant. Engaging. Faith-filled. If you're looking for a book that includes an extraordinary story of devastation and hope, brokenness and victory, along with transparency and transformation—read this book! *Appeal to the Courtroom of Heaven: Petitions for Prisoners and Prison Families* is a book that offers a real-life story of one family's journey. It includes practical understanding of how the justice system works, biblical insight and understanding of how God uses imperfect people, and the added bonus of prayer help-sheets for the challenges we face. This book belongs in every church library, in the offices of Christian counselors, and in the hands of every family member of a prison inmate. Shonda Savage Whitworth offers healing and hope to all who travel this journey.

~ Carol Kent
Speaker and Author
When I Lay My Isaac Down (NavPress)

Appeal to the Courtroom of Heaven stirs emotions but does so much more than that. It infuses families of the incarcerated with the comfort of a listening ear and caring heart—one that has been there. But it›s also a careful and thoughtful comparison between the world›s justice system and what it means to be represented and defended by the Hero of our faith—Jesus. An important read.

~ Cynthia Ruchti
Author of more than thirty books,
including *Ragged Hope: Surviving the Fallout of Other People's Choices* and the award-winning novel
As Waters Gone By, which in part explores the
concerns of the incarcerated and their families

Seldom do I read a work that so engages and challenges me as this one did. Every page is a treasure, and the message of God's grace and mercy shines through from beginning to end. Shonda Whitworth helped me to view God's role as righteous Judge and Christ's role as loving Advocate in a whole new way. Over and over again as I read, I thanked God for what He has done for us through the cross and what He will continue to do for us as we seek His mercy for ourselves and for others. This book isn't just for prisoners and their families; it's for anyone who wants to better understand the privilege we have in appealing to the courtroom of heaven and approaching the throne of grace.

~ Ann Tatlock
Novelist, children's book author and blogger

Shonda and I met at a writer's conference. From the moment I heard her story of God's love and redemption for broken people, I found myself leaning in to discover more about the grace of God. Her book, *Appeal to The Courtroom of Heaven* is a testimony filled with good news. I find her book encouraging and packed with hope. You will too.

~Babbie Mason
Award-winning singer, songwriter, and author

If you completely forgot to study the material for your final exam in biology, you might feel despair when your professor passes out the test. If suddenly your loved one is facing murder charges for a crime they did not commit—and after exhausting all your resources to support his innocence he's found guilty—you will feel despair. Shonda Whitworth felt despair but didn't stay there because she found help at God's throne of grace. In her book,

Appeal to the Courtroom of Heaven, she lays out a unique biblical strategy to pray effectively. If you ever felt hopeless over a loved one facing incarceration, this book must not go unread.

~Gene McGuire
Author of *Unshackled, From Ruin to Redemption*
Chaplain, Babe's Chicken Dinner

Having once been incarcerated, and now after having served full-time in prison ministry for many years since my release, I have read many good books to teach and encourage prisoners but none that were also beneficial to their families. This book abundantly blesses them both! Without hesitation I wholeheartedly recommend Shonda's book as one that is compelling, truthful, practical, helpful, anointed, and potentially life changing. Her teaching on prayer and how to appeal to the courtroom of heaven as applied to prisoners and their loved ones is both unique and instructive. Prayer is our most powerful and effective weapon, and Shonda's suggested prayers are tremendous. Apply these principles. Find hope, healing, and freedom in Jesus.

~Stephen Canup
Executive Director, Freedom in Jesus Prison Ministries
Author of *Jail-House Religion: From Park Avenue... to Park bench... to Prison* and *Diving Deeper: A Daily Leap into a Life More Abundant*

Compelling! Remarkably redemptive and a personal healing experience. Rather than read this book, I prayed through it as it encouraged me, uplifted me, and deepened my relationship with Christ.

~Delores Christian Liesner
Author of *Be the Miracle*

Shonda Whitworth has a great gift from our Lord to communicate and touch the hearts of people for God. When she shared her testimony at the Harvest of Hope Revival in New Mexico, she communicated love and encouragement to the hearts of people who have gone through or are going through similar hurts of having an incarcerated loved one. *Appeal to the Courtroom of Heaven* will bless those who have given up hope or who have been forgotten by the church. Shonda shows the love and care of our Lord Jesus Christ and those who read this book will find real hope.

~Dewey Moede
Pastor
For God's Glory Alone Ministries
https://www.fggam.org/

Having a son that was recently released from prison after serving six years, reading books on how to overcome this kind of pain became my norm. When I read Shonda's book *Appeal to the Courtroom of Heaven*, it was different than other books I had read the past few years. Not only was it engaging, but it made perfect sense. To shift your thinking of what God's plan is in all this is hard; however, it's possible! Prayer is the most powerful weapon we have to fight back, and Shonda explains how to use it effectively. This book is unique and will bring so much understanding to your situation. I suggest anyone living with an incarcerated loved one to read it. It is full of the truth and will change your life when you understand how to appeal to the courtroom of heaven.

~Jodi Calkins
Executive Director, Pioneer Trails Ministries
Advocacy for Incarcerated Loved Ones

APPEAL
TO THE
COURTROOM
OF HEAVEN

Petitions for Prisoners and Prison Families

SHONDA WHITWORTH

Straight Street Books
Lighthouse Publishing of the Carolinas

APPEAL TO THE COURTROOM OF HEAVEN BY SHONDA WHITWORTH
Straight Street Books is an imprint of LPCBooks
a division of Iron Stream Media
100 Missionary Ridge, Birmingham, AL 35242

ISBN: 978-1-64526-252-7
Copyright © 2020 by Shonda Whitworth
Cover design by Hannah Linder
Interior design by AtriTex Technologies P Ltd

Available in print from your local bookstore, online, or from the publisher at:
ShopLPC.com

For more information on this book and the author visit: ShondaWhitworth.com

Unless otherwise noted, all Scripture is taken from the New King James Version®. Copyright © 1982 by Thomas Nelson, Inc. Used by permission. All rights reserved.

Scripture quotations marked (NLT) are taken from the *Holy Bible*, New Living Translation, copyright © 1996, 2004, 2007, 2013, 2015 by Tyndale House Foundation. Used by permission of Tyndale House Publishers Inc., Carol Stream, Illinois 60188. All rights reserved.

Scripture quotations marked TPT are from The Passion Translation®, Copyright © 2017, 2018 by Passion & Fire Ministries, Inc. Used by permission. All rights reserved. ThePassionTranslation.com.

Brought to you by the creative team at LPCBooks: Eddie Jones, Cindy Sproles, Andrea Merrell, and Brian Cross.

Library of Congress Cataloging-in-Publication Data
Whitworth, Shonda.
Appeal to the Courtroom of Heaven / Shonda Whitworth 1st ed.

Printed in the United States of America

Dedication

To my family and friends who have faithfully walked
with us on this unexpected journey.

Acknowledgments

Writing a book about a painful experience has not been an easy endeavor. Yet one of the most beautiful things I discovered in this season is the true love of the body of Christ. In the dark times, the light of Jesus Christ illuminated through many of His precious ones to keep me from being swallowed by despair. Through these trying times, many people have reassured me and helped restore my confidence as I share my testimony. There are too many to list, but I thank you.

To my husband, Eldon—I thank you for sticking with me for better and for worse for over thirty years. I appreciate all the efforts you take to make sure I have time and space to write. I am grateful that you believe in me more than I believe in myself.

To my sons, Stephen and Chase—I am proud to be your mom. I will always love you. God loves you even more than I do, and I look forward to seeing how He uses you both for His glory after this season of preparation.

To my mom, stepdad, and father-in-love—I am grateful for all the loving support and sacrifices you have made through this season. Without your support, I would not be where I am today with a book testifying about all the grace God has bestowed on our family.

To John Thurman and Tama Westman—Just weeks after my son's arrest, you took me to a bookstore, purchased Moleskine® journals, then told me to journal my story because one day I would share it so I could encourage others. At that moment, I could not even comprehend your advice, but I journaled anyway. I will always be grateful for your encouragement to keep writing, especially when I did not want to write.

To Eddie Jones—Since the first writers' conference I attended after my son's arrest, you have encouraged me to write the book and to bleed on the pages. It took me eight years, but I finally wrote the book, and I thank you that you never stopped asking me "Have you written the book?"

To Dewey Moede—I am grateful for your godly wisdom and discernment. Your text messages asking for a post for your ministry site were Holy Spirit inspired and confirmed what He placed on my heart to write at the time. God used you to stir up the gift in me, and I thank you.

To Stephen Canup—I will always be grateful the Lord made our paths cross at the hospitality house when I went to visit my son in prison. From the moment we met, you encouraged me to write. I am thankful for your prayers and your Spirit-inspired-before-the-sun-comes-up phone calls with confirmation.

To my pastors, Ted and Jan Currington—I thank you for encouraging me to follow the Lord's call in ministry and in writing. I would not have pursued the writing of this book or started the ministry without your blessing on it.

To my editors, Cindy Sproles and Andrea Merrell—I thank you for your guidance in putting this book together. Andrea, thank you for helping with the details of the writing craft and cleaning up my work.

And especially to my Lord and Savior Jesus Christ—Thank You for being my Advocate in the courtroom of heaven. Because of You, I freely and boldly approach the throne of grace and receive mercy. Because of You, day by day my hope is renewed, and my wounded heart is being healed. May my testimony bring hope and healing into the lives of many others.

TABLE OF CONTENTS

Foreword

In this book, *Appeal to the Courtroom of Heaven*, Shonda Whitworth presents a profound yet simple truth in which she clearly outlines the steps to obtain spiritual freedom, especially for those she has chosen as her target audience. Her main emphasis is on captives who are behind bars. One thing that makes this book so powerful is that she writes from her own experience—the frustrations and, at times, feelings of hopelessness as her son made bad choices and what those bad choices cost her family, son, and others.

As a result of his choices, her son was found guilty of committing a crime and, as a result, was convicted and is serving a sentence in a state prison. Because of this devastating experience, God led Shonda to begin a ministry to bring hope to prisoners and their families. She took the Scripture seriously that says, *And we know that all things work together for good to those who love God, to those who are the called according to His purpose* (Romans 8:28).

This book describes how there is no hopeless case in God's courtroom. The book clearly explains that God has a plan for every person, whether they might be a prisoner or a victim. It doesn't matter that a person may have messed up their life. God is always ready to extend mercy and grace when we follow His ordained order in the courtroom of heaven. The strategies that Shonda shares to the path of freedom are not just her opinions, they are completely validated in the Word of God, from which many examples are given.

This book is a wellspring of hope straight from the pages of the Bible. It contains God's words spoken to bring encouragement and a sense of expectancy of what God will do in answer to prayer.

When we present our petitions before God, He settles the case in heaven, then it is settled on earth according to Scripture. *Thy kingdom come, thy will be done in earth, as it is in heaven* (Matthew 6:10).

This is a great book and very needed for those who are behind bars and their families. It is well-written, profound yet practical.

-Jeanette Strauss
Author of *From the Courtroom of Heaven to the Throne of Grace and Mercy*

Introduction

What I share in this book kept me going through the process of my son being arrested, convicted, and sentenced to prison. As a mother, these struggles led me to my knees in prayer and compelled me to seek the Lord more earnestly.

When tragedies occur in our lives, we have two choices: turn away from God or run to Him. Should we choose to turn away and resist Him, we then operate in our own strength. As human beings, we don't have the capacity to carry the weight of our trials without assistance. When we turn to the Lord, He carries us and sees us through all trials and adversities that come our way.

There were days when my prayer appeals to the courts of heaven continued all day long. That's because I longed to hear something from God and would not start my day until He spoke to me. I would read the Bible and meditate on the promises of God. Before this tragic event that changed our lives forever, reading the Bible through in a year was my regular practice. I attended Bible studies at church, attended services to hear the preaching of the Word of God, and traveled to Christian conferences to hear mighty men and women of God share the truths from the gospel.

I was already somewhat familiar with the Word of God, but this time things changed in me as I read through the Scriptures. As I sought God, I was transformed. Romans 12:2 tells us that we are not to be conformed to this world, *but be transformed by the renewing of your mind, that you may prove what is that good and acceptable and perfect will of God.* Day by day, I allowed God to transform my mind as I continued to seek Him in His Word.

With new and unexpected experiences in my life, the Scriptures I read were filtered through a different perspective. I realized the Bible is filled with the testimony of people our society would label as thugs and outcasts. And the amazing thing is many of the people Christians call heroes of faith started out as scoundrels. Some of them never served prison time for their crimes. For example, Moses murdered an Egyptian man for mistreating the Hebrew people. He fled to the desert out of fear that Pharaoh would kill him. Yet after forty years of hiding in the desert, the Lord sent Moses back to Egypt to lead an entire nation out of captivity.

Others in the Bible served prison time for crimes they did not commit. Joseph was sold into slavery by his brothers, then falsely accused of attempted rape by the slave master's wife. He was sent to prison on her testimony, but God used that time to refine Joseph's character until it was time to fulfill His purpose (see Psalm 105:19). In today's society, Joseph would be labeled a convicted sex offender. But God used him to interpret Pharaoh's dreams. Afterward, Joseph was promoted to second in command of Egypt.

From Genesis to Revelation, we see how God used liars, cheaters, adulterers, thieves, murderers, womanizers, prostitutes, and prisoners to fulfill His purposes. Reading and understanding how God turned around the lives of messed up people and used them for His glory filled me with hope.

As I read the Bible faithfully every day, not only did I notice how God used prisoners and scoundrels to fulfill His purposes, I also realized the Bible is full of judicial themes. Through my son and his attorney, I experienced the judicial process with the preparations leading up to my son's trial. It continued with the experience of going to trial, the conviction, and sentencing to state prison. That process was a huge learning curve and quite a daunting experience for me.

Yet I never gave up seeking the Lord through it all. A couple of years after the conviction, I wrote and taught a Bible study on The Lord's Prayer called "Powerful and Effective Prayers." As I taught this study at different groups and sought new places to present it, God used a number of people at various times to introduce to me another prayer strategy. This strategy is to pray into the courtroom of heaven.

For the past few years, I've been studying this prayer strategy and implementing it in my own prayer time. This book is a snippet of the understanding I've gained about praying and making appeals to the courtroom of heaven.

This book is not legal advice. It is about praying and making appeals to the highest court of all—the courtroom of heaven. I choose to implore God, who sits on the throne, as we traverse through this journey on earth. Our heavenly Father is also the Righteous Judge. He has final say in all matters both in heaven and on earth. I petition our cases in His court and, in doing so, I have witnessed the Lord turn what the Enemy meant for harm into something good.

This prayer strategy is not a get-out-of-jail-free calling card. God is not a God that can be manipulated so we can get our way. God is sovereign, and we must revere Him as such. We cannot coerce Him or make Him feel sorry for us. God is love, and He loves us more than we realize. His mercies are new every morning.

Even so, God is a just God. Being a just Judge, He must follow His own law, which He laid out for us throughout His Word. God never compromises His truth, and He never renders verdicts that are contrary to His Word. When we allow the Holy Spirit to guide our lives, we no longer desire to live in opposition to God's law, and we live in freedom. If we live our lives according to our own natural desires, we violate God's law, and we enter into spiritual captivity—whether that is literal captivity behind bars or spiritual bondages such as fear, worry, doubt, addictions, anger, unforgiveness, and so forth.

But we have good news. Jesus' finished work on the cross and His resurrection paid our penalty in full. He set the captives free, and He desires for us to live a life in freedom on earth as well as in heaven. Galatians 5:24-25 says, *Those who belong to Christ Jesus have nailed the passions and desires of their sinful nature to his cross and crucified them there. Since we are living by the Spirit, let us follow the Spirit's leading in every part of our lives* (NLT).

After my son entered prison, he experienced true freedom behind bars, which you will read about in the chapters that follow. But my grief and despair over a life I did not imagine placed me in captivity. By God's grace, He did not leave either of us in this captive state. True freedom does not depend on where we live. We experience true freedom when we are led by the Spirit of God.

In the following pages, I share how my son's choices took our family on an unexpected journey and the judicial insights learned in the process. I also reveal some of the biblical prisoners, how the Lord used their lives to change the course of history, and the heavenly judicial system. The first part of this book identifies the most common participants in a judicial setting and the judicial process in both US Courts and heavenly courts. In the second part, we will learn how to silence our accuser and prepare to make our appeals to the courtroom of heaven to seek mercy from the Most High Righteous Judge of all the heavens and the earth on behalf of ourselves and those we love. In the third part you will find prayer petitions for you and your loved ones to appeal to the courtroom of heaven.

Shonda Whitworth

PART I:

The Judicial Process

CHAPTER 1

The Arrest

You really are who you hang out with in this world.
You must surround yourself with the right people.

~ Michael Franzese

My cell phone rang as I prepared for bed at the end of a really happy day. The number on the caller ID reflected a call from my husband's work. It seemed strange that a work call would come to my phone, but I dismissed any premonitions.

The woman on the other end asked for Eldon, who at the time was a federal agent with the U.S. Border Patrol. As he took the phone and listened, he wrote down the name and phone number of a Border Patrol agent in another Texas city.

My thoughts raced. *Stephen, that's where Stephen lives.* The elated mood of the day vanished as a sense of foreboding escalated with each secondhand click.

I stood close by as Eldon sat at the kitchen table and called the number that had been given to him. He was quickly connected with an agent who advised him Stephen had been arrested, and he should contact the local sheriff. My legs weakened, so I pulled out a chair and eased myself into it.

With the sheriff on the phone, my husband looked at me and whispered, "Stephen and Paul have been arrested." Then on a scrap piece of paper, Eldon wrote slowly and in all caps ... M U R D E R.

My heart beat like a drummer tapping out thirty-second notes. Everything around me appeared as if I were on the outside looking in. My mind and body were injected into a nightmare. The remaining conversation my husband had with the sheriff was blocked by the shock that enveloped me.

After the call ended, anguish seized my heart. A young lady's life hung in the balance at the intensive care unit from multiple stab wounds, and a man's life had been snuffed out by bludgeoning. At this point, Stephen and his friend were facing capital murder charges and aggravated assault with a deadly weapon.

"Oh, God, no!" Over and over I pleaded. "Oh, God, no! Don't let this be true!"

This can't be my life, I told myself.

"Lord, please keep that lady alive."

Torment engulfed my emotions. My heart ached for my son. It ached for the victims and their families. I could not process the totality of this horrifying news.

What am I supposed to do now?

Life as I knew it dissolved in an instant. All the checklists I had created to make certain we lived a perfect suburban life no longer mattered. It felt as if someone pulled a string of yarn on the beautiful afghan of my life to unravel it. How could we possibly untangle this mess?

In my despair, a Scripture I heard repetitiously at church when someone faced a difficult situation popped into my thoughts. A Scripture that made me cringe, because it felt so cliché that I didn't want to hear it or even acknowledge it. But what else did I have?

I grabbed a pen and a piece of paper, then opened my Bible to Romans 8:28 and wrote the following words: *And we know that all things work together for good to those who love God, to those who are the called according to His purpose.*

In spite of feeling like this passage has been used to merely gloss over other people's problems, I copied it word for word and clung to it.

Then I prayed, "Lord God, if You are who You say You are, then make this passage true for me and my family and for the families who are grieving tonight. Work something good out of this horrific situation."

I yearned to wake up and thank God it was just a bad dream. But in reality, my life instantly became part of an unimaginable tragedy.

In that agonizing moment, I had to make a choice. Think of God's Word as cliché or choose to believe what He says is real—that with God nothing is impossible, and He can take something reprehensible and work out something for good.

I decided to cling to God's promises. Otherwise, the circumstances would crush me. Jesus is the living Word, and He is our solid foundation.

Functioning on autopilot, Eldon made calls to prepare for the five-hour drive. Since he worked the night shift, he had slept all day and was rested for the nighttime trip. He wanted to be present for Stephen's arraignment scheduled for the next day.

We had recently joined a new church, so I contacted the administrative assistant to notify our pastor, who called and prayed with us. Then a phone call came from a friend in another city. She called to inquire if the Stephen she saw in the news report was our Stephen. That's when I knew the news media across the state was broadcasting this to their viewers. I had to call our family. They needed to hear the news from us first.

Calling family to share this kind of news was an arduous task. With sobs, I merely blurted out, "Stephen is alive, but he's been arrested for murder."

I cried on the phone with my brother first, then my mother. I had nothing else to explain to them as we did not know the full extent of the circumstances. The not knowing left my imagination open to run amuck.

After surrendering our lives to Christ, Eldon and I attended church regularly and practiced what other godly parents practiced. Our aspiration was for our boys to do well in school, earn a college degree, find gainful employment, marry a godly woman, and have children.

We celebrated God's love together in church and in the home. Both of our boys professed Christ as their Savior at early ages and followed in water baptism.

Believing we did everything parents are to do to train up a child in the way he should go—so when he is old, he will not depart from it (see Proverbs 22:6)—we celebrated Stephen's high school graduation and looked forward to the next phase of life for him.

Stephen chose to work full time in lieu of going to college. He moved into his own apartment. Once Stephen lived on his own, I had no control over the choices he made, who his friends were, or what he did with those friends. As a mother, I continued to point out the dangers of sketchy friendships.

Stephen lived a prodigal lifestyle, but I prayed in faith, believing he would soon return home just like the prodigal son in Luke 15. Other parents of adult children whose sons and daughters entertained a lifestyle of smoking, drinking, and drug use encouraged me that Stephen would come to his senses. Their stories stirred my faith as their sons and daughters left that scene without having encounters with the law or, at a minimum, misdemeanor cases.

Just nights before Stephen's arrest, I had asked the leader of a home group Bible study to pray for Stephen. She said, "Don't worry, Momma. He'll be fine."

But this was *not* fine. It looked like my son would never be home ... ever again.

Due to the ongoing investigation, the sheriff's department could not inform us of the details that led to our son's arrest. But we knew Stephen was with a friend whom we had warned him about repeatedly, and now he was in serious trouble.

Stephen had no prior arrests and, to my knowledge, no traffic tickets. Our life with our son jumped from no trouble with the law to the most serious trouble possible. Granted, his friendships were questionable, but I never dreamed anything this tragic would unfold.

Unimaginable.

In Judges we learn about Samson, an Israelite man dedicated to God from his birth until his death. Samson came along at a time when the Israelites rebelled against God, and the Lord allowed the Philistines to oppress them for forty years.

During this season of Philistine oppression, an angel of the Lord appeared to Manoah's wife and informed her—though she had been unable to conceive—she would give birth to a son. This son was to be dedicated to God from birth, and she was instructed that he was not to *drink wine or any other alcoholic drink nor eat any forbidden food* (Judges 13:4 NLT). His hair was never to be cut.

When Samson became an adult, he decided to marry a Philistine woman. His parents spoke out against his choice and desired for him to marry an Israelite woman. Samson insisted on marrying the Philistine.

At the wedding celebration, Samson made a bet with thirty men for thirty fine linen robes and thirty sets of festive clothing to see if they could solve his riddle during the seven days of celebration.

Stumped, the thirty men approached Samson's wife and enticed her to pry the answer from him. They threatened to burn down her father's house if she did not get the answer for them. She nagged Samson until he told her. Then she shared the information with the men.

Samson knew how they obtained the answer. So, out of anger, he killed another thirty men and took their belongings to pay his debt. Then he left his wife and returned to his father's house.

After his temper abated, Samson returned to his wife, only to learn her father had given her to another man. Once again, Samson's outrage flared up. He tied together the tails of 300 foxes in pairs and set them on fire to run through the grain fields, vineyards, and olive groves destroying all the Philistine crops. As punishment against Samson, the Philistines burned Samson's wife and her father to death.

Furious, Samson vowed to take revenge on the Philistines. He attacked and killed a great number of them before running off to hide in a cave.

The Philistines searched for Samson by setting up camp in Judah. The men in Judah inquired about the attack. They informed Judah they only wanted Samson. The men of Judah found Samson and convinced him to surrender so they could turn him over to the Philistines.

When they saw Samson bound with ropes, the Philistines shouted in victory.

> But the Spirit of the Lord came powerfully upon Samson, and he snapped the ropes on his arms as if they were burnt strands of flax, and they fell from his wrists. Then he found the jawbone of a recently killed donkey. He picked it up and killed 1,000 Philistines with it. (Judges 15:14-15 NLT)

After the elation of his victory wore off, Samson fell in love with Delilah.

> The rulers of the Philistines went to her and said, "Entice Samson to tell you what makes him so strong and how he can be overpowered and tied up securely. Then each of us will give you 1,100 pieces of silver." (Judges 16:5 NLT)

Delilah pleaded with Samson to tell her the secret of his strength. Every time I've read this story from the Bible, I wonder why Samson did not recognize the pattern of behavior as his first wife begged for information—which did not turn out well.

Three times Delilah attempted to lure the information from him. Three times, he tricked her and the Philistines by overpowering them. But then she went to him with her best sullen face and said, "How can you tell me you love me if you don't share your secrets with me?"

Day after day, Delilah badgered him to tell her his secret.

> Finally, Samson shared his secret with her. "My hair has never been cut," he confessed, "for I was dedicated to God as a Nazirite from birth. If my head were shaved, my strength would leave me, and I would become as weak as anyone else." (Judges 16:17 NLT)

Knowing Samson told her the truth this time, she called the Philistines back, lured Samson to sleep, and they cut off his hair. Samson's strength left him. When the Philistines overtook him, he attempted to shake them off. But the Lord had left him.

So, the Philistines captured him and gouged out his eyes. They took him to Gaza, where he was bound with bronze chains and forced to grind grain in the prison. (Judges 16:21 NLT)

Delilah merely used Samson for personal financial gain. Three times she attempted to overpower him by learning his deepest secret: the source of his strength. Perhaps all the years of overcoming the Philistines caused Samson to feel invincible.

Samson's relationship with Delilah led to his demise— losing his eyes, his freedom, and ultimately his life. Samson comingled with his enemies, the very people God assigned him to conquer.

When we enter into a relationship with others, whether an intimate relationship or a casual friendship, we begin to think and behave like them. All of us are influenced by other people. We need to associate with those we desire to emulate. My son's questionable friendships led to an unimaginable tragedy that resulted in his arrest.

Arrest means "to seize (a person) by legal authority or warrant; to take into custody."[1] Once arrested and confined to jail, the individual enters into the judicial system as a defendant to face the consequences—alone. Known friends often scatter and usually are not anywhere around to avoid being caught or implicated themselves. The lifestyle and relationships that lead to an individual's arrest cease to exist while confined.

Donald Miller, author of *Father Fiction: Chapters of a Fatherless Generation* (Howard Books) wrote:

> Last month I visited a prison in Texas. I had the chance to guest-teach a class in a progressive rehabilitation program. I taught, but mostly I listened. As the guys told me their stories, their reasons for being in prison,

I noticed a common thread. The real reason they were in prison was not because they had committed crimes, though they had, but rather it was because of the people they hung out with. Almost all problems and success in life boil down to relationships. These guys had gotten themselves into relationships that led to trouble. Either they had joined gangs or hung out with drug addicts or met girls who took them down a bad path. The reason they were in prison was because their friends, in a way, put them there.[2]

Even if not physically confined, our lives can be arrested. Another definition of arrest means "to check the course of; stop; slow down." If our lives are not progressing and we feel stuck, there is a possibility our relationships may be hindering our spiritual development.

Wherever we are in life—whether we're living on the outside in the free world or inside the barbwire chain-link fences—we have a choice in the relationships we choose. The relationships we have will influence us positively or negatively. Proverbs 13:20 warns us, *He who walks with wise men will be wise, but the companion of fools will be destroyed.*

We need to ask ourselves if our relationships will help us grow to be wise and more Christlike. Or if our relationships are foolish ones that will lead us on the path of destruction and separate us from our heavenly Father.

No one has to be a slave to a person, gang, or affiliation. For those who feel trapped in those lifestyles, if you will choose to surrender yourself to Christ, He will show you a way out of those ungodly alliances. His Word is filled with promises, such as one found in Proverbs 16:7: *When people's lives please the* LORD, *even their enemies are at peace with them* (NLT).

How's that for a promise? Even those who hate us because we choose to separate ourselves from them will live at peace with us when we live our lives to please the Lord.

If our present relationships pull us away from God, we need to sever them and seek new friendships with those who will encourage us to pursue God.

CHAPTER 2

The Defendant

*The apostles Paul and Peter and the prophet Jeremiah all went to
prison because they knew God. I came to prison to know God.*

~ Rico Johnson[1]

In Texas there are only two sentencing options for capital
crimes: life without parole and the death penalty. Even in my
state of shock upon learning about this tragedy, my thoughts
fixated on my son's eternal condition. Regardless of what
consequences he faced in this world and my grief over what
was to come, my primary concern was that he would not cross
over into eternity separated from God.

As Eldon prepared to leave for his five-hour drive, I penned
a note for Stephen in the event Eldon could pass it along. I
scribbled *We love you.* And then I wrote out the Scripture about
God's forgiveness. *If we confess our sins, He is faithful and just
to forgive us our sins and to cleanse us from all unrighteousness* (1
John 1:9).

Based on God's Word, if Stephen confessed his sins, God
would forgive him. Even if my son lived separated from family
in this lifetime, I longed for the assurance we would all be
together as a family in the next.

The following day, Eldon was permitted to see Stephen.
The sheriff allowed him to give the note to our son.

Later that afternoon, my phone rang, displaying an unknown number on the caller ID. With jittery fingers, I answered and heard a recording that announced a collect call from an inmate. My heartbeat reverberated loudly in my ears as I fumbled to press the correct numbers to accept the call. Finally, we were connected.

"Mom, I love you. I only have five minutes."

What do you say when there's only five minutes? "You got my note?"

"Yes, I love you. Mom, I did not do this!"

I urged Stephen not to talk about anything that happened on the phone or in the jail. I explained we were looking into hiring an attorney for him.

In an attempt to be brave and strong for him, I forced my voice through a dry throat and mouth and shared with him the hope we have that God would turn things around. Five minutes seemed like a few seconds. We exchanged another round of "I love yous" before the call was disconnected.

Some relief came after hearing my son's voice, though temporary, for then a fountain of tears poured out of me. Thoughts pulled my emotions in opposing directions. My unconditional love for my son and my need to support him wrestled with how he could be involved in the loss for one man's family and severe injuries to a young woman.

Stephen and his former friend, now co-defendant, were both charged with first-degree felony for murder and second-degree felony for aggravated assault with a deadly weapon. Bond was set at 1.25 million for each.

Thankful the death penalty no longer applied, life in prison still remained a possibility. All the dreams for my oldest son to live a productive life, find a godly woman to marry, and have a family shattered like a crystal vase on a tile floor. Now, with the tiny fragments and sharp shards of my desires for my family scattered across the room, the only way to exit this nightmare was to walk barefoot across my broken dreams to reach the door of hope.

As his mother, I could not imagine my son capable of something so heinous and brutal. But the nightmare remained. The tragedy engulfed me like a tidal wave as I recalled the distress I heard in his voice. Night after night as I attempted to sleep, movies played in my mind about what could have possibly unfolded that catastrophic night. I would wake up hot and sweaty, screaming out in horror. Every time, my husband embraced me tightly, comforting me until it passed.

While detained in the county jail, the investigation against Stephen and the judicial process began its course. We called bail bondsmen to inquire about the possibility of bailing Stephen out of jail. We learned that even if we had the finances or found a way to obtain them, none of the bondsmen we spoke with would even consider it, as it was too much of a risk for them.

When Stephen's attorney filed for a bond reduction, it was denied. The prosecution argued that we lived in a border town with Mexico, and Stephen was a high flight risk. The judge agreed, so Stephen remained in county jail.

Stephen's confinement detached him physically from those who loved him. And his communication was limited to twenty-minute phone calls and handwritten letters. Stephen was placed in segregation where he was not allowed to work or go to recreation with the general population inmates. Being alienated from other people forced Stephen to reflect on his choices.

Stephen's incarceration in county jail necessitated that we learn about a whole new world we knew nothing about. We found out we needed to place funds on a commissary account for him. Undergarments and certain personal hygiene items were not provided by the county but were allowed to be purchased by inmates through the commissary system. In order to write letters, Stephen needed to purchase paper, pens, and stamps. Also, having the funds to purchase snack foods gave Stephen some sense of normalcy in an abnormal world.

I could no longer send a text or call my son when the urge struck me to reach out to him. Forced to wait until Stephen was allowed to call me, I treasured every minute we spoke. We talked at least once a week for the twenty minutes preprogrammed by the jail's telephone system. Since all the calls were recorded, we refrained from talking about the events that unfolded that fatal night. Yet with so many unanswered questions, it took a great amount of discipline to find other things to share.

In my conversations with Stephen, I chatted about our daily activities and reiterated my faith in God to work all things out for good and that, somehow, He would turn this around. I asked Stephen, "Have you recommitted your life to Christ?"

"Ah, Mom, I don't know if I want jailhouse religion," Stephen said. He related how he didn't want his conversion experience to be perceived that he was bargaining with God to get out of jail. He expressed concern about how it would appear to the attorneys.

"If it's a true conversion experience, what does it matter what others think?" Both Eldon and I emphasized to Stephen that this tragic situation was a wakeup call for him to get his heart right with God. Otherwise, his life would never improve.

With the uncertainty of what Stephen's future held—and not being able to fully reason with him about his need for a Savior in twenty-minute conversations once a week—I wrote him lengthy letters five days a week. In those letters, I shared the gospel message of hope.

After learning from the jail mailroom how to send books, I ordered an easy-to-read translation study Bible with footnotes, commentaries, and maps. I did all a mother could to saturate Stephen in God's Word. While he spent his pretrial months in segregation, it was my desire for him to have a personal encounter with God through the Holy Bible.

Two months after Stephen's arrest, I received a letter from him regarding his decision to surrender his life to God. He wrote:

> I have been doing a lot of thinking about what you said about letting God have control. You know I am a stubborn person and don't like not having control, but after much thought and prayer I have decided to give my life to God. I'm praying that He help me through this and help to make my life better than what I made it. I wish I could have made better choices in my life, and I feel like I let y'all down by making the wrong choices, but I will try and make up for it. I love y'all and miss y'all so much! Thank you for helping me through this, I hope I will get to hug you soon. Love, Stephen

Due to wrong choices, the Lord removed Stephen from all that was familiar to him. With the time Stephen had to contemplate, he surrendered his life to the only One who can guide him to make better decisions.

Accused of crimes, Stephen became a defendant in the judicial system. In county jail, he repented and asked Jesus to be his Savior. I was comforted with the fact that no matter what our future held, my son's eternal salvation was secure, and he would get to know God better through the process. As a family, we proceeded through the judicial process with an understanding that God is in control of our future.

After my son's arrest, as I read the Bible, I saw the Scriptures from a different perspective. Now, the scandalous lives of biblical characters leapt off the page at me.

I noticed that many of our heroes of faith were what many in our society deem unworthy. The Bible contains plenty of examples of those who had criminal behaviors but were redeemed and restored to be used in mighty ways by the Lord.

I found one such wicked person whom the Lord redeemed tucked away in 2 Kings 21 and 2 Chronicles 33. After the godly king of Judah, Hezekiah, passed away, his son Manasseh replaced him as king. Manasseh did not follow in his father's footsteps but set up pagan altars and worshipped false gods.

Manasseh murdered his own sons to sacrifice to the false gods. *He practiced sorcery, divination, and witchcraft, and he consulted with mediums and psychics. He did much that was evil in the Lord's sight, arousing his anger* (2 Chronicles 33:6 NLT). He *murdered many innocent people until Jerusalem was filled from one end to the other with innocent blood* (2 Kings 21:16 NLT). In today's terms, he would be known as a mass murderer or a terrorist.

Under Manasseh's leadership, the people of Judah were convinced to follow his example. The country was amuck with crime and perversion.

The Lord sent prophets to King Manasseh and to the people of Judah to warn them. Yet they ignored God's admonition (2 Chronicles 33:10). Therefore, the Lord allowed the army of Assyria to take Manasseh prisoner. *They put a ring through his nose, bound him in bronze chains, and led him away to Babylon* (vs. 11).

God orchestrated circumstances to separate Manasseh from all the evil that was familiar to him. In this separation, Manasseh could no longer listen to the negative influences in his life. As a result, *while in deep distress, Manasseh sought the Lord his God and sincerely humbled himself before the God of his ancestors* (vs. 12).

Guess what happened next? God listened to Manasseh and was so moved by his sincere and humble pleas that He released Manasseh from prison. Not only was he released from prison, he was reinstated as king of Judah. Imagine the uproar and outrage our society would raise if a convicted mass murderer was released back into our community and reinstated as our ruler. Would we believe he truly surrendered his life to the Lord and expressed true humility?

We do not know how long Manasseh remained in prison before being released. But during the time he was imprisoned, Manasseh had an epiphany. He *finally realized that the Lord alone is God!* (vs. 13).

Due to his encounter with the one true God while incarcerated, when Manasseh returned to his kingdom, he removed all the foreign gods and idols. He tore down all the altars that he erected in the temple. He reinstituted the proper sacrificial offerings and worship to the Lord. Manasseh's actions proved he was truly repentant.

The Lord separated Manasseh in order to get his attention. Captivity was his wake-up call, which led Manasseh to humble himself before the Lord. Then the Lord restored him to his kingdom where he reigned for a total of fifty-five years. Interestingly, we find in the first chapter of Matthew, Manasseh's name listed in the genealogy of Jesus Christ.

Reflecting on the biblical account of Manasseh filled me with hope. Hope that if God would restore a king as evil as Manasseh who lived under the old covenant, then through the redemptive work of Jesus Christ in the new covenant there is even greater hope for my son, who has humbled himself in repentance, to be restored to his family.

Even in the midst of the condemning accusations against my son and the impending trial, I found comfort in knowing that no matter the ramifications, Stephen's salvation was secure, and his lifelong relationship with the Lord had begun.

Scripture shows us that God uses captivity to draw people unto Himself. The captor, or defendant, has a choice to humble himself before the Lord or resist. There is hope for redemption and restoration when we choose to get to know God through His Son, Jesus. It is better to face the accusations from the prosecutor with the Lord.

CHAPTER 3

The Prosecutor

The major strategy of Satan is to distort the character of God and the truth of who we are. He can't change God, and he can't do anything to change our identity and position in Christ. If, however, he can get us to believe a lie, we will live as though our identity in Christ isn't true.

~ Neil T. Anderson

Prosecutors review evidence in criminal cases to determine whether the case should be brought to trial. According to the American Bar Association, the prosecutor's role is "to seek justice, not merely to convict."[1]

A prosecuting attorney must hold a Juris Doctor degree, pass the state bar exam, and be elected or appointed by the government to the position. Most prosecutors obtain legal experience in private practice prior to seeking an appointment or running for election.[2]

Both the district attorney and assistant district attorney sought to bring justice to the victims and their families. What the families suffered was devasting.

With my husband as a law enforcement officer and my prior experience working with federal law enforcement, we understood the need for justice. Yet now we were torn. It was our son who faced prison time for being involved in something deplorable. Of course, we never imagined that something like this would happen. What parent does? We experienced a great deal of emotional conflict as we searched for the proper balance between the need for justice on behalf of the victims and their families with the unconditional love we have for our son.

Based on the surviving victim's statement, the prosecutor had suspects in custody, and they were ready to prosecute to the full extent of the law. Though the news media ran the initial story statewide, the district attorney ordered the documents in the case sealed. With this order, no one would see the gruesome investigation unfold in the media, which protected the victims and their families as well as our family.

As Stephen sat in the county jail awaiting trial, the investigation against him continued. The prosecutor commissioned the investigators to seek more evidence in order to strengthen their case against the accused.

The prosecutor sought a grand jury indictment against Stephen. In Texas, grand jury proceedings, which are closed to the public, determine if felony charges should be brought against the suspect of a crime.[3]

The grand jury consists of twelve eligible men and women subpoenaed within the county in which they live. Only the district attorney (DA) representing the state is allowed to present the case to the jurors. The DA may call in witnesses to testify if necessary.

In Texas, the defendant has no right to know that a grand jury is considering the case or even to participate in the proceedings. To receive an indictment, nine of the twelve grand jurors must be convinced there is enough probable cause to indicate the defendant is guilty. This is known as "true-bill."[4]

After Stephen received an indictment, both the prosecutor and the defense team began their work to prepare for trial. There were several pretrial hearings. We did not attend these hearings due to the distance.

A pretrial hearing is where the judge determines if the defense is ready for the trial, if they have access to all the evidence, and if they have had a chance for an independent investigation[5]. And this is the time the defense reviews the state's evidence. Also, the prosecutor reviews pertinent information in order to propose a punishment for the accused. Sometimes there may be several hearings before any negotiations are made. If neither side reaches a plea agreement, the case will be scheduled for trial.[6]

The DA presented Stephen's attorney with a plea deal for fifty years for the murder and twenty years for the aggravated assault, with the sentences to run concurrently. The offer was only on the table up to the first pretrial hearing. If not accepted, it would be withdrawn.

We received the following email from Stephen's attorney the week prior to the scheduled pretrial hearing:

> The October pretrial is scheduled for 10:00 a.m. You do not need to be there for the pretrial, but I am sure Stephen will want to talk to you about the plea offer. I do not think this is a good offer, however, the DA has stated that she believes she has a very good case against both Stephen and [the codefendant]. Stephen told me that he wants to reject the offer.

Fifty years sounded like a lifetime. I was not even fifty years old, so the thought of my son living behind bars that long felt like a brick wall collapsed on me. When we had an opportunity, we briefly discussed the options with Stephen on the phone. With a jury, they could decide within the sentencing range of five to ninety-nine years.

What if he goes to trial and is sentenced anywhere from fifty to ninety-nine years? I wondered.

We shared with him that the decision was his to make, but we agreed with the attorney that it was not a good offer.

Stephen declined the plea bargain offer and requested a trial by jury. We believed that when all the relevant information Stephen's attorney shared with us came out in court before the jury, Stephen would be able to come home with us after the trial.

During the time from the arrest leading up to the trial, the investigators searched my son's background for any past criminal records, activities, or misconduct of any type. Stephen had no prior record with the law, so the investigators examined his past for unsavory character traits.

I recommitted my life to Christ when Stephen was in elementary school. As parents, my husband and I enrolled Stephen in Christian schools to ensure he received a Christian education as his foundation.

By the time Stephen was in eighth grade, we were in a position that allowed me to resign from work and be a stay-at-home mom to both our boys. I homeschooled the boys to lay the foundation of Christian heritage. We lived on a block with four other homeschooling families with children in the same age range. Social activities, as well as group study activities with these families, were scheduled every week.

We attended church regularly as a family to reinforce the Christian values we taught in our home. We celebrated the love of God both at church and at home. Both boys professed Christ as their Savior at a young age, followed by water baptism.

As a teenager, Stephen volunteered with the children's church leaders on Sundays. He loved playing with the children and working with them in the classes. After he was no longer able to attend Vacation Bible School in the summers, he assisted the VBS volunteers. By the time he was fourteen years old, he was placed in charge of small groups during the annual week-long activities.

At sixteen, Stephen accompanied me and a team from our church on a two-week short-term mission trip to Cameroon, Africa. Stephen had a knack for traveling and adapting to different cultures. He ministered to the children in Africa, and the ministry leadership in Cameroon shared how they saw a missionary calling on his life.

As Stephen's high school teacher, I geared his curriculum to prepare him for junior college or a trade school. He scored well enough on exams and learned concepts easily, but he worked better in small environments. As a tactile learner, Stephen preferred to be doing things. I envisioned him working in a trade career after high school.

As his parents, my husband and I believed we started Stephen's life on the right course by laying a solid foundation on Christ, setting him up for a successful life as an adult.

After Stephen graduated from high school with nineteen hours of college credits, he decided to work full-time and live on his own in lieu of attending college. He worked various low-income jobs.

Searching for better employment opportunities, Stephen scored very high on the Border Patrol entrance exam. He was selected and was in the process of the background investigation when he befriended the codefendant. With the lure of making more money than one can earn with the federal government, he declined the government job to seek employment opportunities in the oil field industry in a community five hours from where we lived. With this quest, he became involved in a decadent lifestyle.

Our life choices testify about our good character or our moral corruption. Stephen turned away from the ways we taught him after his high school graduation. As an adult living on his own, he failed to follow the Christian foundation we instilled in him in his youth. Stephen believed lies from the Enemy that distorted his thoughts, which led to wrong choices. Though he was influenced by a friend, the real Enemy was and is not of flesh and blood.

> For we are not fighting against flesh-and-blood enemies, but against evil rulers and authorities of

the unseen world, against mighty powers in this dark world, and against evil spirits in the heavenly places. (Ephesians 6:12 NLT)

Though the real Enemy is spiritual, we are accountable for our choices in the natural realm. The prosecutor probes the defendant's past in search of anything and everything to justify a conviction and the maximum sentence allowed under the law in order to seek justice. Stephen's choices were counted against him in the prosecutor's investigation.

———————

In the earthly courts, the prosecutor seeks justice, but in the heavenly courts the prosecutor is unjust. We frequently refer to him as the Devil, the Enemy, or Satan. In Scripture he has two distinct titles: accuser and adversary.

Revelation 12:10 tells us that the accuser brings accusations against us before God, not just occasionally, but day and night.

> Then I heard a loud voice saying in heaven, "Now salvation, and strength, and the kingdom of our God, and the power of His Christ have come, for the accuser of our brethren, who accused them before our God day and night, has been cast down."

The word *accuser* in the Greek is *kategoros*. It means "a complainant at law; spec. Satan—accuser."[7] Scripture shows us how, as an accuser, Satan asks to take each of us to trial.

> And the Lord said, "Simon, Simon! Indeed, Satan has asked for you, that he may sift you as wheat. But I have prayed for you, that your faith should not fail;

and when you have returned to Me, strengthen your brethren." (Luke 22:31-32)

In this passage, Satan accused Peter and asked for him to be brought to trial. The words "asked for" mean "to demand the freedom of" and "to demand the surrender of."[8]

Just like the earthly prosecutor looks into the defendant's past history, the heavenly accuser keeps records of all our wrongs. Every white lie spoken, every deceitful scheme to get our own way, every foul word used against someone, every peek at immoral images, and so on. The Enemy keeps them all recorded in his books.

When a believer petitions the Lord for an answer to a situation, the Enemy files his opposing petition in the courtroom of heaven, presenting evidence as to why we are not qualified to receive answers to our prayers. Those reasons are based on the record of our wrongs, which are unconfessed sins. When we cover up our sins, it will never go well for us. But in confessing them, we will find mercy. Proverbs 28:13 says, *People who conceal their sins will not prosper, but if they confess and turn from them, they will receive mercy* (NLT).

Satan is also called our adversary. Matthew 5:25 tells us, *Agree with your adversary quickly, while you are on the way with him, lest your adversary deliver you to the judge, the judge hand you over to the officer, and you be thrown into prison.*

The word *adversary* in the Greek is *antikidos,* meaning "an opponent in a lawsuit."[9] Satan seeks ways to oppose all our petitions before God. Since false testimonies are not admissible in the courtroom of heaven, when the accuser brings an accusation against us, it is true. We need to agree with him and repent.

In her book, *From the Courtroom of Heaven: Prayers & Petitions*, Jeanette Strauss writes:

We can't be foolish enough to think this prosecuting attorney doesn't have a file on each of us that contains the truth concerning sins that we have committed. (This may be the only time he is interested in truth). This testimony of sin, which he will use against us in front of the Judge, will give him the strength to convict us and effectively divert us from the case we came to present. The accuser (prosecuting attorney) is in position, ready and waiting with testimony of our sin. "The sting of death is sin; and the strength of sin is the law" (1 Corinthians 15:56).

It is wonderful for the Righteous Judge, our Lord, to be able to respond to him with these words, "This saint's case has been expunged. He has repented for his sins and asked forgiveness, placing them under the blood of My Son, so they have been cleansed by the blood. Their sin is no more. Next case."[10]

When we understand the Enemy's tactics and the accusations he will take before the Judge based on our poor lifestyle choices, we can remove those offenses and have them deleted from our record in the courtroom of heaven by seeking our Advocate, confessing, repenting, and placing the sinful deeds under the blood of Jesus. This process is explained in more detail in Chapter 9, Silencing the Accuser.

The prosecutor in the heavenly court diligently prepares a list of our wrongs. His primary strategy is to lead us away from God so that we will live in opposition to Him. The adversary uses schemes to ensnare us, so he has the right to dispute our petitions.

The accuser knows the Word, which is the law in the courtroom of heaven, better than many believers. That's why it is important for us to seek the Lord daily in His Word so we know His will for us. When we do not seek to understand the ways of the Lord, we fall prey to following a path that leads to moral corruption, and the heavenly prosecutor presents our immoral choices before the Righteous Judge.

Just as we have a right to legal defense in the earthly courts to counter the prosecutor's accusations against us, the Righteous Judge provided an Advocate to represent us in the courtroom of heaven.

CHAPTER 4

The Defense Attorney

Mercy and grace are always available to us if we break God's law.
All we need to do is call on Christ our Advocate!

~ Kenneth E. Hagin

Unable to sleep the night we received the news of our son's arrest—and with my husband on the highway on his way to see Stephen—I called a friend, hoping she would answer a middle-of-the-night phone call. Thankfully, she did.

I informed her of our desperate situation. For several hours through my sobbing, she encouraged me during that dark moment. She emphasized that we would want to seek adequate legal counsel. I kept reiterating how we could not afford that kind of attorney. She reassured me there is always a way.

A defense attorney represents the accused. Other titles for a defense attorney are lawyer, advocate, barrister, and counselor. This representative is authorized by the state to practice law, which means they can give legal advice to clients, draw up legal documents, and represent the client in a court of law. An attorney's primary role, whether in a criminal or civil case, is to protect the client's interest.

Since we had never hired a criminal defense attorney before, we had no idea what we were doing. After Eldon arrived in the city where Stephen was arrested, he met with one of the detectives on the case. He was informed that he would not be allowed to be present during the arraignment, but would be permitted to see Stephen afterward. While waiting, Eldon decided to look for an attorney in order to gather some information.

As we talked on the phone later, we were uncertain if we should spend money on a defense attorney for Stephen or allow him to be represented by a court-appointed attorney. Eldon asked around the community for a list of attorneys but hit a dead end.

Struggling to find a recommendation for a criminal attorney, Eldon called me again. Since I was at home, I opened up the Google browser and searched for attorneys. The list on the page populated, and I read off the names.

When I came to the address of a certain attorney, Eldon said, "That's the street I'm on, and I'm parked in front of that building." Stressed and with little sleep, we had no idea if this was the right direction or not, but we took it as a sign from God.

Eldon spoke with the legal assistant in the office, who explained the difference between using a court-appointed attorney and hiring a private attorney.

A court-appointed attorney is randomly selected. Their services are at no cost to the client or the family. We were told we would not know the quality of the attorney's work or his workload. Since their workloads are usually overextended, many of these attorneys are known for bargaining for plea deals to avoid the lengthy trial preparation and jury trials.

To hire a private attorney requires a significant retainer for representation due to the large number of hours required to work on a criminal case. A private attorney is believed to commit more time on a case than a court-appointed attorney, because the workload is spread out with legal assistants, private investigators, and access to other types of services to aid in preparing a defense.

The private attorney at that office was not available to meet with Eldon that morning, but an appointment was set for them to meet later in the afternoon after Stephen's arraignment.

We continued to wrestle with the representation issue. Stephen qualified for a court-appointed attorney, but we had no idea who that would be and if they would be devoted to the case. Details about Stephen's case were unknown, as it was too soon and under investigation. But we imagined it would be complicated.

Eldon and Stephen visited with one another face-to-face after the arraignment. Able to look at Stephen directly in the eyes and read his body language, Eldon determined that Stephen needed private representation.

Eldon returned to visit with the attorney we randomly picked from the Google search, and I was connected into the meeting via speakerphone. Neither of us knew what questions to ask, but the attorney spoke in a calm and soothing voice to explain the legal process. He informed us that he had twenty-eight years of experience. Then he mentioned how in tragic cases like this, there are misunderstandings and details that can be sorted out through the investigation. He explained that if what Stephen said was true—he was there but did not commit the crimes—he felt confident he could get a not-guilty verdict or probation.

The fees for this type of case were disclosed. We knew attorneys were costly, but we were not prepared for the disclosure of such a significant expense. They kindly offered suggestions for ways to acquire that kind of money, such as taking out a second mortgage, refinancing a vehicle, taking out a loan, borrowing from a retirement account, or a combination of those means.

When Eldon returned home, we discussed our financial options. Six years prior to this situation, my husband and I filed personal bankruptcy due to a failed business venture. The year before this tragedy, we purchased a home and dealt with the bankruptcy explanations in order to secure a mortgage loan. To apply for a new loan while the bankruptcy still appeared on our credit report meant we would once again have to explain, *plus* reveal the reason we needed these funds. This caused a great amount of emotional distress and embarrassment.

Since we agreed that we wanted our son to have the best legal representation possible, we felt we had no other option than to apply for a loan. The attorney made us feel comfortable about hiring him to represent Stephen. Eldon described the Bibles he saw lying around the office and how the attorney and his staff professed to be Christians. The staff shared encouraging Scriptures whenever we called to ask questions. Since our priority was to obtain the best legal counsel possible, and we were encouraged by this attorney, it did not cross our minds to consult with other lawyers.

With the title to our truck in hand, we walked into our credit union to visit with a loan officer. Somehow, we managed to remain in control of our emotions and explain our situation as matter-of-factly as possible. After explaining our botched credit history and our plans to repay the loan, within an hour we secured the needed finances and wired the large retainer to the attorney.

Once again, especially in light of our credit history, we believed the Lord gave us another sign we were on the right track. I comforted myself with the knowledge that Stephen now had a defense attorney to look after his best interests during the investigation and judicial process.

Criminal legal representation for my son came at a hefty price. My husband and I made sacrifices to ensure he had quality legal counsel. We prayed the Lord would use this costly defense attorney to advocate for Stephen's freedom.

To become an attorney in the United States, one must complete a bachelor's degree, pass the Law School Admission Test (LSAT), attend law school, then pass a state bar exam. There is also a character evaluation. Only three states ban convicted felons from becoming attorneys—Kansas, Mississippi, and Texas. All the other states will consider an applicant based on how the applicant's lifestyle has improved since the conviction.[1]

In the kingdom of God, only one person is qualified as an Advocate in the courtroom of heaven. Jesus met the Father's qualifications. He lived a life without sin to fulfill the law, and then completely surrendered His will to the Father's will, even accepting the death penalty when He did not deserve it.

When Jesus took His seat at the right hand of the Father, He became the one and only qualified Advocate in the courtroom of heaven.

> My dear children, I am writing this to you so that you will not sin. But if anyone does sin, we have an advocate who pleads our case before the Father. He is Jesus Christ, the one who is truly righteous. (1 John 2:1 NLT)

As our Advocate, Jesus relates to us in every possible way. He understands everything we go through and more. Yes, even the convict and their families. *This High Priest of ours understands our weaknesses, for he faced all of the same testings we do, yet he did not sin* (Hebrews 4:15 NLT).

Jesus was betrayed by one of those in his inner circle who received a payment of thirty pieces of silver. Then Jesus was arrested in the middle of the night and taken to be interrogated. This included thirty-nine brutal lashes to His back.

During this interrogation, His remaining friends scattered. Peter denied knowing Him three times before the rooster crowed, just as Jesus told him would happen.

After His arrest and beating, Jesus stood before Pilate as an innocent man. Pilate knew Jesus had done no wrong, but he caved to the political pressure by the public to release a known criminal and sentence Jesus to death. Jesus stood by silently as the execution order was given.

Through this unfair trial and sentencing, Jesus yielded to His Father's will. Before Jesus' arrest, He petitioned His Father to "remove the cup" from Him, yet God the Father, also the Righteous Judge, remained silent.

The death sentence given to Jesus was carried out immediately with no opportunity for any appeals. The decision was sealed. Already suffering from the beatings from the Sanhedrin, Jesus was escorted to the execution site as the crowds mocked Him. The execution took place on a cross in front of a multitude of witnesses.

Jesus suffered cruel and unusual punishment during His execution. Nails were hammered through His hands and feet to a wooden cross. Then the cross was raised to allow His life to slowly seep out of Him.

As Jesus hung there, the crowds continued to mock Him. They cast lots for his robe, vying for His earthly possessions as He died. With life draining from His body and His blood spilling on the ground, Jesus said, *Father, forgive them, for they don't know what they are doing* (Luke 23:34 NLT). Jesus forgave those who wrongfully persecuted and mocked Him as He took His last breaths.

A soldier punctured Jesus' side with a spear. After the executioners confirmed His death, Jesus was removed from the cross and buried in a borrowed tomb. His family, friends, and the community grieved over His death. They not only grieved the loss of a family member and friend, they grieved over the loss of their hopes for a king to change their present circumstances.

Joseph of Arimathea, who had become a disciple of Jesus, asked Pilate for Jesus' body. When Pilate agreed, Joseph wrapped Jesus' body for burial and placed Him in a newly purchased tomb. He sealed the tomb with a stone, and Pilate ordered that the tomb be guarded by soldiers.

There was division among the people. They either rejoiced at His death, believing they rid themselves of their problem, or they mourned deeply as they believed all their hope in the future of their country died with Jesus.

Three days later, the stone that sealed the tomb was rolled away. The grave was empty. Death lost its power to the resurrection power of our Lord.

Jesus is alive, well, and seated at the right hand of the Father.

Jesus met the qualifications to be our Advocate in the courtroom of heaven, and the cost for this representation has already been paid in full. To acquire His representation, all we have to do is ask for Him.

Without Jesus' representation, we will be judged according to the sins that the prosecutor presents to the Righteous Judge.

Jesus, our Advocate, paid for all our wrongs and received our penalty. He paid for our ransom by the shedding of His blood.

> He canceled out every legal violation we had on our record and the old arrest warrant that stood to indict us. He erased it all—our sins, our stained soul—he deleted it all *and they cannot be retrieved!* Everything we once were in Adam has been placed onto his cross and nailed permanently there as a public display of cancellation. (Colossians 2:14 TPT)

By accepting Jesus' free representation in the courtroom of heaven, our record of wrongs is expunged, and we are made righteous before the Lord. To ask Jesus to be our Advocate, we acknowledge we are a sinner, believe that Jesus is Lord, and confess this truth with our mouth. When we do, all our sins are nailed to the cross as a *public display of cancellation.*

Asking Jesus to be our Advocate is as easy as A-B-C. Here's how.

Admit You Are a Sinner

Everyone who does not live a life in perfect obedience to the Lord is guilty of sin and subject to the death penalty. None of us can plead "not guilty" in the courtroom of heaven. Romans 3:23 says, *For we all have sinned and are in need of the glory of God* (TPT). We all have a need for Jesus' righteous representation. Making this admission humbles us before the Lord. Humility positions us to receive God's forgiveness, grace, and mercy.

Believe Jesus is the Son of God

For this is how much God loved the world—He gave His one and only, unique Son as a gift. So now everyone who believes in Him will never perish but experience everlasting life. God did not send His Son into the world to judge and condemn the world, but to be its Savior and rescue it! (John 3:16-17 TPT). When we believe God provided salvation through His Son, Jesus Christ, we receive the gift of eternal life.

Confess Jesus as Lord

We must declare that Jesus is Lord. Romans 10:9-10 says, *For if you publicly declare with your mouth that Jesus is Lord and believe in your heart that God raised Him from the dead, you will experience salvation. The heart that believes in Him receives the gift of the righteousness of God—and then the mouth confesses, resulting in salvation* (TPT). When we confess that we believe

Jesus is Lord with our mouth, meaning we tell others about our belief, we surrender our lives to Him, giving Him authority over us. We then have the desire to do His will, not our own.

If you believe and are ready to ask Christ to be your Advocate, here's a sample prayer.

> Father God, I acknowledge that I am a sinner and do not measure up to Your righteous standard. I deserve to be separated from You, but I thank You for making a way for me to be reconciled to You. I believe You sent Jesus Christ, Your only begotten Son, who lived a perfect life so that He paid my penalties and received my judgment on the cross. I believe He was raised up on the third day and now sits at Your right hand as my Advocate. Today, I confess Jesus as my Lord and Savior, turn from my independence, and surrender my life completely to You. I repent of my sins and ask for forgiveness and cleansing. I ask You to fill me with the Holy Spirit to empower me with Your grace to live my life according to Your will. Thank You, Lord, for my new life and Your promise that I will live in heaven for all eternity with You. In Jesus' name, Amen.

Congratulations! If you prayed the prayer to ask Christ to be your Advocate, I encourage you to share this good news with a chaplain or a pastor and to find a church congregation that will help you grow in your faith.

With Jesus as your Defense Attorney, you can confidently enter into the courtroom of heaven to find mercy and grace instead of judgment.

CHAPTER 5

The Judge

A holy God made the universe in such a way that actions true to His character, and the laws derived from His character, are always rewarded. Actions that violate His character, however, are always punished. He rewards every act of justice; He punishes every act of injustice.

~ Randy Alcorn, *The Purity Principle* (2003)

In the judicial process after an indictment, a judge is assigned to a case. The judge presides over all proceedings, including all preliminary hearings, pretrial activities, and the trial itself. In trials by jury, the judge gives the panel of jurors instructions to follow while deliberating the case. In some trials, the judge, instead of a jury, decides the case. If found guilty, the judge may also determine the defendant's sentence.

During the process leading up to a trial, if the defense attorney or the prosecutor desires a specific action be made, they must present it to the judge. For example, if the defendant's attorney seeks a bond reduction on behalf of the accused, a petition is presented to the court with the request. A hearing is then scheduled before the judge where both the defense and the prosecutor proffer their reasons for or against the bond reduction. The judge makes the decision.

In a case where the defendant selects a trial by jury, the judge presides over the trial to ensure that both parties and the witnesses follow proper courtroom procedures. This is designed to make sure the trial is a fair one.[1]

Evidence gathered against a defendant must be legally obtained. The judge determines if any evidence that either parties desire to present is illegal or improper. The government cannot use any evidence obtained through an illegal search, seizure, arrest, or interrogation. Certain protocols are set in place that must be followed for these to be considered legal to be presented in the trial.[2]

The judge decides if witness testimonies are considered misleading or hearsay. And the judge determines whether or not to allow expert and character witnesses to testify. [3]

At the time we retained the attorney, we were informed that for criminal proceedings like this it took one to two years before moving into trial. Yet in Stephen's case, the prosecution stated they were prepared and ready to proceed as quickly as possible.

Since Stephen declined the DA's plea bargain offer, a trial by jury was scheduled. Initially, my son's trial was to take place six months after the tragedy. But it was postponed several times as Stephen's attorney filed motions to fully prepare a defense.

In one of the meetings with Stephen's attorney prior to the trial, we agreed to hire an expert witness to complete a psychiatric evaluation on Stephen and to have the expert testify at the trial. The prosecution had a doctor prepared to testify about Stephen's condition and state of mind, so we agreed it would be beneficial to have a second opinion presented before the jurors.

Stephen's trial commenced nine months after his arrest. The jury selection process started on a Monday morning. Selecting a jury was an ordeal as most of those in the jury pool presented reasons for not wanting to be on the panel. I could relate to them as I've done the same when I sat on jury panels.

My husband and I were allowed to observe the jury selection process and to hear the opening statements by the prosecution and the defense. Listening to these opening statements, we were hopeful about the direction of the trial.

Since both Eldon and I were character witnesses, we were not allowed to sit inside the courtroom during the trial. We were informed that we would be able to return for closing arguments.

Thankfully, the court provided a private room for us across the hall from the courtroom where we waited during the trial. I was grateful to be secluded in a room with a table and chairs, out of the public's view. The state's witnesses, the victims' family and friends, and the media, waited in the chairs that lined the hallway outside the courtroom.

Since the burden of proof lies with the prosecution, they presented their evidence and called their witnesses against Stephen first. The state's primary witness was the young woman who survived the tragedy from that horrific night. For two and a half days, the prosecutors presented their evidence before the jury.

Finally, on Thursday, Stephen's attorney began to call witnesses. When he called for the expert witness to testify, the prosecutor objected and presented information to the judge as to why he should not be allowed to testify. Stephen's attorney argued why he should be allowed. Unfortunately, the judge sided with the prosecution to not allow the doctor to present his evaluation of Stephen during the guilt/innocence phase of the trial. Stephen's attorney came into the room where we waited and informed us that the doctor would not be allowed to testify. He sent him on his way.

As I watched the doctor leave the room and get on the elevator to go down, my already heavy countenance dropped lower as I saw the lights above the elevator door count down, indicating the doctor reached the first floor.

Other defense witnesses were called in to testify. Then my husband was called into the courtroom. I sat and prayed while he was in there. After Eldon returned, it was my turn. While walking forward, I kept my eyes ahead of me and tried not to notice all the people watching me.

Seated in the chair on the witness stand, I kept my eyes on Stephen's attorney, not sure where else to look. I answered questions related to Stephen's character and childhood and was grateful when the prosecutor passed on cross examination. I was dismissed and eager to return to the safety of our waiting room.

During a recess, Stephen's attorney came into our room and said, "The judge will not allow the defense of acting out of fear or necessity."

"What?" I blurted. I was shocked. Dazed. Appalled. My hope for a positive outcome in this trial sank like a stone thrown into a lake.

"The judge not allowing the duress defense is grounds for an appeal," the attorney said.

With my hope descending into the lake of despair, I did not want to consider an appeal. The appellate process takes years, and rarely are the lower courts' decisions reversed. I believed in the judicial system and wanted this jury to hear the whole truth. Yet the judge ruled that the jury would not hear the duress defense.

Late Thursday afternoon, both the state and the defense rested. The judge ordered a recess until Friday morning. When we returned on that morning, we sat inside the courtroom behind Stephen and listened to the closing arguments. Two prosecuting attorneys collaborated against Stephen, who only had one attorney representing him. The state presented first, then the defense. The state's attorney wrapped up with final comments to the jury. After the presentations were finished, all I could do was pray and hope for my son's future.

In criminal trials with a jury, the judge gives specific instructions to the jurors and explains the laws that apply to the case as well as the standards that must be used in making the decision about the defendant.[4]

After the closing arguments were finished, the judge read the charges against Stephen to the jurors and gave them their instructions. The court recessed that morning at 10:10 a.m. while the people who held my son's fate in their hands went into deliberation.

After about five hours, the jury returned with a verdict.

Guilty on both counts.

The judge's decision to not allow the duress defense was disheartening. While I do not excuse any part of my son's role that traumatic night, I admit I had expectations for the court to present the whole truth for the jury to consider while deliberating. Later, I learned from reading the trial transcript that when the attorneys argued before the judge whether or not to allow the expert witness and the duress defense, the jurors were not present in the courtroom.

I'll always wonder if there would have been a different outcome if the judge had allowed the jury to hear the portion of testimony about my son's duress that horrific night and to hear the defense's professional medical evaluation by a doctor to counter the prosecution's medical review before the jury.

After my son's trial, I realized that in most trials, facts are presented, but the whole truth is not made known to the jury. Both sides, the defense and the prosecution, petition the judge to prohibit information to be presented that will hinder their desired outcome. The judge's role is to determine what can legally be presented in the court. Often, there are myriad conditions around the defendant's life and the circumstances that the jurors are not allowed to consider during deliberation. Jurors make decisions based solely on the testimony and evidence the judge allows in the courtroom.

Because of my faith in God, I hold no ill will toward the judge that presided over Stephen's trial for excluding the duress defense and the expert witness' testimony. God is in control of all things, including the judges of this earth. Stephen's trial was covered in prayer by me, his father, other family members, and many other intercessory prayer warriors.

Since the establishment of the law for the Hebrew nation, the Lord set the bar of expectation for those who judge. Judges were instructed not to twist the law, show any type of partiality to one person over another, accept gifts or bribes, or twist the words of the truth.

The following two Scriptures were recorded in Leviticus and Deuteronomy for how judges were to carry out justice in the newly formed Hebrew nation. *Do not twist justice in legal matters by favoring the poor or being partial to the rich and powerful. Always judge people fairly* (Leviticus 19:15 NLT). *You must never twist justice or show partiality. Never accept a bribe, for bribes blind the eyes of the wise and corrupt the decisions of the godly* (Deuteronomy 16:19 NLT).

The first appointment of judges is recorded in Exodus 18. Since the exodus of the Hebrew people from Egypt, Moses judged cases from morning to evening. His father-in-law, Jethro, visited and noticed his fatigue. This is the wisdom Jethro shared with Moses:

> So, Moses' father-in-law said to him, "The thing that you do is not good. Both you and these people who are with you will surely wear yourselves out. For this thing is too much for you; you are not able to perform it by yourself. Listen now to my voice; I will give you counsel, and God will be with you: Stand before God for the people, so that you may bring the difficulties to God. And you shall teach them the statutes and the laws, and show them the way

in which they must walk and the work they must do. Moreover, you shall select from all the people able men, such as fear God, men of truth, hating covetousness; and place such over them to be rulers of thousands, rulers of hundreds, rulers of fifties, and rulers of tens. And let them judge the people at all times. Then it will be that every great matter they shall bring to you, but every small matter they themselves shall judge. So it will be easier for you, for they will bear the burden with you. If you do this thing, and God so commands you, then you will be able to endure, and all this people will also go to their place in peace. (Exodus 18:17-23)

Moses took his father-in-law's advice and set up a court system to make judicial decisions based on the law. He chose judges who were trustworthy and hated bribes. These judges were to decide on the small matters, but the greater matters were presented to Moses.

The Lord expects earthly judges to be impartial to the best of their ability, but the human nature continually resurfaces. In Luke 18:1-8, Jesus shared a parable about an unrighteous judge and a persistent widow. Repeatedly, the widow sought justice with this judge in a dispute with an enemy. This judge ignored her for quite some time, *but finally he said to himself, "I don't fear God or care about people, but this woman is driving me crazy. I'm going to see that she gets justice, because she's wearing me out with her constant requests!"* (vs. 4-5 NLT).

Jesus went on to explain this parable. If the widow woman could get a righteous verdict from an unrighteous judge, how much more will God our Righteous Judge give His own people justice when we cry out to Him?

Earthly judges are fallible. This is why we must seek the Lord for justice, not man. *For the Lord is our judge, our lawgiver, and our king. He will care for us and save us* (Isaiah 33:22 NLT).

In Daniel 7: 9-10, we read about a vision Daniel had of God the Judge sitting on His throne. This is the closest we have to a visual picture of the Righteous Judge.

> I watched till thrones were put in place,
> And the Ancient of Days was seated;
> His garment was white as snow,
> And the hair of His head was like pure wool.
> His throne was a fiery flame,
> Its wheels a burning fire;
> A fiery stream issued
> And came forth from before Him.
> A thousand thousands ministered to Him;
> Ten thousand times ten thousand stood before Him.
> The court was seated,
> And the books were opened.

Ancient of Days refers to God as a chief Judge. God our Father is also God our Righteous Chief Judge who is seated on His throne in the heavenly court. In Hebrews 12:23, He is referred to as *God, the Judge of all.*

Every one of us will have our final day in the courtroom of heaven. We all will stand before the Righteous Judge to receive a verdict. The question is … are we ready for the eternal judgment day?

CHAPTER 6

Judgment

This prison wasn't God's judgment on my life; it was His mercy.
If I would have kept going the way I was living, I would have
ended up in hell for eternity.

~ A famous evangelist, quoted in *Driven by Eternity*

T
hrough all the months leading up to the trial, Stephen's attorney revealed information and evidence to us that, though Stephen was there, he was not the one who performed the heinous offenses against the victims. After our son was convicted, the attorney explained the Texas Law of Parties to us.

The Texas Law of Parties is a penal code of "Criminal Responsibility for Conduct of Another." This law does away with the distinction between accomplices and principals. In other words, a person is criminally responsible for an offense if he intentionally aided, assisted, solicited, encouraged, or failed to try to avert the offense.[1]

With this new insight, a fresh wave of emotional distress consumed me. *Why weren't we told about this law before the trial? Why are we learning about it after my son's conviction?*

The tiny bit of hope remaining in my tank drained out with the tears that poured over my cheeks. First, the jury was not allowed to hear the necessity out of fear and duress testimony. Second, the expert witness was not allowed to testify about

Stephen's state of mind. And now, this information about the law that the jurors were instructed to follow swallowed me like a tsunami and left me drowning in despair.

With several hours remaining on that Friday afternoon, the judge proceeded right into the sentencing phase of the trial. In Texas, in noncapital felony cases, the defendant must decide prior to the trial if he is convicted whether he wants to be sentenced by the judge or by the jury. Stephen chose to be sentenced by a jury.

During the punishment phase, both the prosecution and the defense called witnesses to testify about the convicted. This is the portion of the trial where everything about the person's past is presented and laid bare—whether good or bad. Past employment history, psychiatric evaluations, and character witnesses testify.

The prosecution team called their witnesses first. Then the defense attorney called Eldon to testify. I followed. Stephen's attorney asked me questions about how I homeschooled, what type of curriculum I used, about Stephen's volunteer work teaching children's church, and about our short-term mission trip to Africa. When he passed me to the prosecution, she said she had no questions.

As I stood up to leave the witness stand facing the juror's box, filled with so many emotions, I whispered a prayer. "Please have mercy."

The prosecutor stood up and shouted, "Objection, your honor!"

The DA marched toward the bench, and Stephen's attorney joined her. The bailiff came to my side and gently guided me by my arm away from the bench. I looked over at Stephen. His face was soaked with tears and distorted with grief and agony. Seeing my son like that caused anguish to swell up in my body and forced the tears to burst out of my eyes.

Once back in the safety of our waiting room, I chastised myself for not maintaining my composure. I prayed and hoped

I had not made things worse for Stephen. So many questions raced through my mind, and I tried to turn them into prayers.

What don't I understand? What do the jurors think? Will any of us ever fully know what happened that night? Does the victim know about Stephen's duress? The families? There's so much misery and distress for everyone present. The victims experienced so much loss. Lord, comfort them. Bring healing to them. Will they ever be able to forgive Stephen? Lord, You forgave my son of his sins, and we will have eternal life together. Will we ever be together again in this lifetime? Will you release him from captivity as I thought You showed me? Lord, who can understand Your ways? You are a God of justice and mercy. The victims' families seek justice against him. We all deserve justice, yet in Christ we receive mercy. Lord, will you have mercy on Stephen in this life?

Shortly after my testimony, the judge recessed court until Monday morning when Stephen's expert witness would testify. We waited out the weekend not knowing the fate of our son. The jurors had all weekend to ponder and process their thoughts. Eldon and I packed our things and returned home for the weekend.

Unable to talk to Stephen before we left town, I had no idea what he was thinking or feeling as he sat alone in a jail cell. I prayed for the Lord to meet him there. To encourage him, strengthen him, and give him hope in the midst of despair.

Back at home, we broke the news of Stephen's conviction to our youngest son, Chase, and Eldon's father who stayed with Chase that week. Our pastor met us at our house and prayed with us. It was a dose of comfort to our anguished souls. On Saturday morning, Chase played a baseball game in spite of his personal heartache. Despite my own mental and emotional distress, I sat in the stands to watch his game and show support for him.

Normally, I socialize with people easily. That day I struggled to be pleasant with others at that early morning game and avoided conversation by hiding under a ball cap and dark sunglasses. Detached from the world, I watched as others around me smiled, laughed, shouted, cheered, and jumped up and down. Life for those around me continued while my world had stopped. My hopes for my oldest were dashed, and I could not find any joy in the moment.

On Sunday, we attended our home church. The praise and worship team sang JJ Heller's song, "Love Me" that has a verse describing a man sitting alone in his jail cell crying out to God and God's response to him. My emotions erupted in the midst of corporate worship. I sobbed, picturing my son alone in his cell crying to the Lord. Thankfully, the pastor recognized my need and asked the congregation to gather around me and my family to pray for us. It brought me a great deal of comfort to have so many loving people surround us, pray over us, and tell us they love us.

After church, we made the five-hour trek back to where the trial was located. We decided that we all needed to be together as a family for this life-altering proceeding, so Chase and my father-in-law accompanied us. My mother met us there, as she traveled from a different city. We all arrived early enough on Sunday afternoon to have a video visitation with Stephen.

Seeing the peace Stephen had on his face and hearing how he had not lost his faith strengthened my resolve to not give up hope. He spoke in a matter-of-fact tone and said, "We continue to trust and have faith in God." What a turnaround. My convicted son spoke words of encouragement to me.

We returned to the courtroom on Monday morning to resume the sentencing phase of the trial. When the expert witness arrived, the punishment phase of the trial resumed. After the doctor's testimony, the trial moved to closing arguments. At this point, we were allowed into the courtroom.

Stephen's attorney asked the jury to consider probation with restitution, making him responsible instead of warehousing him in a state facility. The prosecution, of course, requested the jury to give Stephen the full sentence of ninety-nine years.

After hearing the closing arguments, the jury was once again given instructions to follow while deliberating their decision for sentencing.

My family and I gathered in the waiting area outside the courtroom set aside for us. We talked and prayed. After almost three hours of deliberation, the jury returned with a decision.

We filed into the courtroom and sat behind the defense table. The victim's family sat behind the prosecution. Two sheriff's deputies positioned themselves on each side along the bar inside the gallery.

Before calling for the jury to return to the courtroom, the judge admonished those of us who were seated. "Ladies and gentlemen in the gallery, just a reminder to you, this is a court of law, and I will expect you to conduct yourself with decorum while you are here. Any outbreaks will be subject to contempt of court."

With the deputies' presence towering over me, I sat as still as a statue. My youngest son held my left hand and my husband held my right hand. Numbness crept over me, freezing me into position. My mind processed the motions of the court like watching a movie in slow motion.

The judge asked the jury foreman for the decision. The bailiff took it from the foreman and handed it to the judge. The judge looked at it, folded it, and handed it back to the bailiff, who in turn handed it back to the foreman.

The judge said, "Mr. Whitworth, will you please stand?"

Stephen and his attorney rose from their seats. As the foreman started reading the verdict, Eldon squeezed my hand. My heart resounded loudly in my ears, but I could not hush it. Our eyes were on the jury foreman.

"Verdict of the jury for the offense of murder … twenty years. Verdict of the jury for the offense of aggravated assault … twenty years."

The judge thanked the jury for their service, then dismissed them. After the jurors left the courtroom, the judge officially pronounced the judgment of two concurrent twenty-year sentences against Stephen.

After the sentence was read, I prayed silently. *Twenty years, Lord. You promised me my son will be released from captivity. Even if it takes twenty years, he will be released. Thank You.*

When court was adjourned, the bailiff emptied the courtroom, but asked me and my family to remain seated. He locked all the doors. With only Stephen's attorney, Stephen, and our family in the courtroom, we were granted the favor of spending a few precious minutes with our son around the defense table while the bailiff and attorney sat in the jurors' box by the door.

We hugged. We cried. We apologized. We said we loved one another. We had not had physical contact with Stephen prior to his arrest, and it would be several more months before we could again until he was processed into the Texas Department of Criminal Justice (TDCJ) system. We were allowed to take pictures with Stephen. This was a bittersweet moment. We gathered together in a circle, held hands, and prayed to our Father in heaven, the Righteous Judge, before they took Stephen through the door to live life as a prisoner.

Judgment day was over. Even in my despair and as awful as things were, I knew it could have been so much worse for Stephen. Life was worse for the victims, and I still struggled to reconcile my unconditional love for my son with the grief I felt for their families.

The judgment rendered against Stephen for his role in the offenses committed was twenty years. The Bible tells us that each one of our lives will be judged—both for the believer and the unbeliever. Everyone will face a judgment day.

When life as we know it ends, whether by our passing or when Jesus returns, God will judge all people. *We will all stand before the judgment seat of God* and *each of us will give a personal account to God* (Romans 14:10,12 NLT). Everything about our lives will be examined in the courtroom of heaven.

The choices we make in this lifetime define where we live in eternity. There is no end to eternity; it's everlasting. God is called the *Everlasting Father* (Isaiah 9:6), and He placed eternity on our hearts (Ecclesiastes 3:11). God is the Righteous Judge (Psalm 7:11), and He set a day that He will judge the world (Acts 17:31).

Eternal Judgment

In *Driven by Eternity,* John Bevere wrote:

> The judgments to be made that day are called *eternal* (see Hebrews 6:2). In other words, the decisions made that day—which will be based on how we aligned our lives with God's eternal Word—will determine how we spend the rest of eternity. There will never be any changes to those decisions, for they are eternal *judgments.*"[2]

This eternal judgment is referred to as the Great White Throne judgment. It is the final judgment at the end of the Millennium for all who rejected the message of God, including Satan.

> And I saw a great white throne and the one sitting on it. The earth and sky fled from his presence, but they found no place to hide. I saw the dead, both great and small, standing before God's throne. And the books were opened, including the Book of Life. And the dead were judged according to what they had done, as recorded in the books. The sea gave up its dead, and death and the grave gave up their dead. And all were

judged according to their deeds. Then death and the grave were thrown into the lake of fire. This lake of fire is the second death. And anyone whose name was not found recorded in the Book of Life was thrown into the lake of fire. (Revelation 20:11-15 NLT)

Pat Robertson explains it like this:

According to the Bible, the great books recording the deeds of all mankind will be opened. Those people whose names were not recorded in the "book of life" will be cast into the lake of fire reserved for the devil and his angels. This experience is called "the second death" to distinguish it from mere physical death."[3]

This means eternal separation from God. Theologians differ on what the books contain, but based on first century history, many speculate the books contain the events of each person's life. When a criminal was crucified, they nailed a piece of paper to the cross with the basis for his conviction. Pilate posted above Jesus, *Jesus of Nazareth, the King of the Jews* (John 19:19). Prisoners' crimes were posted outside the cells so all would know why they were there.[4]

On judgment day in the courtroom of heaven, those books will be opened if a person's name is not written in the Lamb's Book of Life. To have our name written there, we must confess Jesus as our Lord and Savior. Jesus said, *I tell you the truth, those who listen to my message and believe in God who sent me have eternal life. They will never be condemned for their sins, but they have already passed from death into life* (John 5:24 NLT).

True believers in Christ will not be judged at the Great White Throne Judgment, for Christ paid for their sins on the cross.

Judgment Seat of Christ

Believers in Jesus will appear before the Judgment Seat of Christ. *For we must all appear before the judgment seat of Christ, that each one may receive the things done in the body, according to what he has done, whether good or bad* (2 Corinthians 5:10).

Jesus will be the Judge over our lives. From the moment we believe in Christ, we become accountable for every word we say and the way we choose to live. Our lives will be evaluated on how well we used the gifts and talents given to us. Our works will be judged.

Our works will not save us. Only receiving Jesus as our Savior secures our salvation. But once saved by grace, we must serve the Lord with our works. We are builders who build on the foundation that Christ laid. First Corinthians 3:12-15 says:

> Now if anyone builds on this foundation with gold, silver, precious stones, wood, hay, straw, each one's work will become clear; for the Day will declare it, because it will be revealed by fire; and the fire will test each one's work, of what sort it is. If anyone's work which he has built on it endures, he will receive a reward. If anyone's work is burned, he will suffer loss; but he himself will be saved, yet so as through fire.

On this judgment day in the courtroom of heaven, our works will be tested by fire. The worker whose works demonstrate value will receive a reward. The worker whose works burn up will not be rewarded, but will still be saved.[5]

As believers, we must examine our lives to see how we line up with the Word of God. He has plans and a purpose for each of us. We are responsible to be certain we fulfill the calling the Lord has for us.

Temporal Judgments

Lastly, we will examine God's temporal judgments—the earthly judgments that happen in this lifetime. This judgment is a form of discipline used to correct us, but only after we fail to adhere to the warnings God gives us. He allows the consequences of our actions to fall upon us. God is sovereign, just, and fair.

The Bible is filled with examples of God's judgments. When studying the Word, we see that the judgments are progressive, from stern warnings to more severe. God allowed the consequences of choices to come upon individuals or corporately as a nation.[6]

As you have already read in previous chapters, the Lord uses imprisonment as a form of discipline as seen in the lives of Samson and King Manasseh. As a nation, the Lord allowed Judah to be taken into captivity by the Babylonians, because the people failed to heed His warnings. The Lord spoke through His prophets and told Judah they would live seventy years in captivity.

Through the prophet Jeremiah, they were instructed to build homes, plant gardens, marry, and have children. God promised at the end of the seventy-year sentence, they would return home. He gave them this promise:

> For thus says the Lord: After seventy years are completed at Babylon, I will visit you and perform My good word toward you, and cause you to return to this place. For I know the thoughts that I think toward you, says the Lord, thoughts of peace and not of evil, to give you a future and a hope. Then you will call upon Me and go and pray to Me, and I will listen to you. And you will seek Me and find Me, when you search for Me with all your heart. I will be found by you, says the Lord, and I will bring you back from your captivity; I will gather you from all the nations and from all the places where

I have driven you, says the Lord, and I will bring you to the place from which I cause you to be carried away captive. (Jeremiah 29:10-14)

God wanted their hearts and knew it would take captivity for them to call upon Him. When they did, He released them to return to their homeland. God is always faithful. We can read about their return and restoration in the prophets of the Old Testament.

The Lord desires for us to respond to the prompting of the Holy Spirit and initially make right choices. When we disregard the nudge—that many refer to as our conscience—the Lord allows us to suffer the consequences of our choices to get our attention so we will turn back to Him in repentance.

Temporal judgments are the consequences of our choices. It is a form of discipline that leads us to a place of repentance if we ignore or fail to recognize the conviction of the Holy Spirit. God disciplines those He loves. *My child, don't make light of the Lord's discipline, and don't give up when He corrects you. For the Lord disciplines those He loves, and He punishes each one He accepts as His child* (Hebrews 12:5-6 NLT).

When we live according to the Spirit, we obey the laws and live in freedom. When we choose to disobey the laws, there are consequences, both in this natural world and in the spiritual realm.

In hindsight, I realize now that my son's conviction and imprisonment were a result of God's mercy. God answered my plea and extended mercy to Stephen. If Stephen had continued on the path he chose before his arrest and conviction, he may have never truly sought a relationship with the Lord and would have been doomed for eternity.

CHAPTER 7

Appeal

For if I am an offender, or have committed
anything deserving of death,
I do not object to dying; but if there is nothing in these
things of which these men accuse me,
no one can deliver me to them. I appeal to Caesar.

~ Apostle Paul, Acts 25:11

The following day after receiving judgment—and without hesitation—Stephen's attorney filed a notice of appeal. In Texas, the deadline to file a notice of appeal is thirty days after the judgment is signed.

The trial attorney cannot be the appeal attorney. Therefore, Stephen needed new legal representation. Having exhausted our finances, Stephen requested an appointed counsel to represent him in the appellate process. A first appeal is a constitutional right, and the state granted him an appointed attorney.

Moving forward, the appellate process crawled like a snail. The newly appointed attorney needed time to review the twelve volumes of the trial transcript. Appeals can only be made on errors that occurred during the trial, not any missing information or opinions on what should have happened.

After months of studying the transcripts and case law and recognizing the complexity of Stephen's case, the appeal attorney filed for three extensions with the court of appeals. Each time the extension was granted. Though slow moving, I continued to pray about the appellate process.

In the meantime, we entered into our new world of understanding the Texas penal system. Stephen was transferred into the Texas Department of Criminal Justice (TDCJ) system. Once again, we had to learn how to operate in a different world that felt like a foreign land. Because prison security is a high priority, the procedures for setting up telephone accounts, visitation lists, and commissary accounts are complicated.

Several months after the conviction, Stephen arrived at the intake prison facility. At this point, we were allowed to have our first prison contact visit with him. Other than those few minutes we were granted by the bailiff after the trial, this was the first time we had been able to touch him since before his arrest. And this was the first time we could talk to him without our conversations being recorded.

At the first state prison, Stephen continued to grow in his faith in the Lord, and he requested to be water baptized. A few months later, Stephen arrived at a transfer facility. He lived at that prison until the state decided which prison unit they would use to house him. At the transfer unit, Stephen enrolled in the General Education Development (GED) class.

Since Stephen graduated high school as a homeschool student, TDCJ would not recognize the unaccredited diploma, nor would the state accept the notarized transcript used for college admissions. In prison, Stephen took all the required GED classes and scored very high on the final exam. With his GED diploma and the nineteen hours of college credit, he was classified eligible to take college classes should he ever be housed at a prison that offers college courses.

We established new routines for phone calls based on Stephen's class and work schedule. We continued our weekly letter writing routine. Since visiting Stephen required us to travel six hours, we scheduled visits two or three times a year.

To remain in consistent communication with one another, we relied on our telephone conversations and handwritten letters.

Nine months after the judgment was rendered against Stephen, the appeal attorney filed the brief with the appellate court. He found four points of error from the trial that he presented before the higher court. These points are related to the same points the trial attorney told us about during the trial—two points on the basis of not allowing testimony of the defense of necessity and two points related to the defense of duress.

The state filed their rebuttal brief three months later. Then we waited for the appellate court justices to review the case. After two years and two months from the time Stephen was sentenced, an appellate court decision was rendered. They wrote in their decision:

> We affirm the judgment of the trial court as to Appellant's conviction and punishment for murder. We reverse the judgment of the trial court as to Appellant's conviction for aggravated assault with a deadly weapon, and we remand the cause to the trial court for further proceedings on that charge.

One conviction was reversed by the appellate court, the other upheld. The reversed case was returned to the DA, who made a decision not to prosecute the case again but dismissed it.

Since Stephen was sentenced to two twenty-year sentences to run concurrently, this reversal by the appellate court did not change his prison release date or parole eligibility date. It merely reduced the number of convictions on his record.

Following this decision, the appellate attorney filed a petition of discretionary review (PDR) for the case to be reviewed by the Court of Criminal Appeals in Austin. The following year, the highest appeal court in the state affirmed the lower appeal court's ruling. Presently, the conviction stands.

My faith in God's promises to redeem and restore His children, including my son, stands firm. Through the judicial process with my son, I learned to believe God's promises and to trust Him with our lives, but not to set up expectations in how He will fulfill them. Day by day, I choose to serve the Lord with joy and gladness through this season of my son's incarceration.

Stephen petitioned the state appellate courts as allowed by law. He sought opportunities to use the legal options available to him, combined with prayers as an appeal to the courtroom of heaven for his release.

In Acts 21-28 we find the journey of the Apostle Paul to Jerusalem, to prison, and on to Rome. Paul had been on a mission trip throughout much of Asia, where he preached the gospel. Now, Paul had a desire by the Spirit to return to Jerusalem and then go to Rome (Acts 19:21).

Paul already knew things would not go well for him in Jerusalem. *And now I am bound by the Spirit to go to Jerusalem. I don't know what awaits me, except that the Holy Spirit tells me in city after city that jail and suffering lie ahead* (Acts 20:22-23 NLT).

On this journey toward Jerusalem, the word from the Lord to Paul was confirmed through others in Caesarea. A man by the name of Agabus from Judea showed up and prophesied to Paul. *The Holy Spirit declares, "So shall the owner of this belt be bound by the Jewish leaders in Jerusalem and turned over to the Gentiles"* (Acts 21:11 NLT).

All of Paul's friends begged him not to go to Jerusalem. But Paul insisted and said, *Why all this weeping? You are breaking my heart! I am ready not only to be jailed at Jerusalem but even to die for the sake of the Lord Jesus* (Acts 21:13 NLT).

Paul arrived in Jerusalem and was welcomed warmly by fellow Christians. But after hearing about his missionary work, they shared with him the accusations he faced from the Jerusalem believers—how he turned his back on the Jewish customs and taught that other Jews were to stop following the Law of Moses. In order to prove the rumors were false, the elders instructed Paul to go to the temple, join in the purification ceremony, and observe all the Jewish laws.

The next day, Paul joined the other men at the temple in the purification ritual. About a week into the process, some Jews from the province of Asia incited a riot against Paul with accusations that he desecrated the temple. The crowd dragged Paul outside the temple and attempted to kill him. The Roman soldiers responded to the uproar, and the crowd stopped beating on Paul.

A Roman commander arrested Paul and began an inquiry as to what he had done. There was too much confusion, so the solders took him to the military base for questioning. Upon arrival at the military headquarters, Paul asked for permission to speak to the Jews. The commander granted Paul's request.

Paul motioned for the crowd to hush. Then he spoke, offering his defense to the horde. He explained that he was a Jew, educated under a well-known rabbi, and passionately served the Lord just as they did. So much so, that he persecuted the Christians, delivering them to prison and harassing them to the point of death.

Paul continued to relay his conversion experience on the road to Damascus. How Jesus knocked him to the ground, spoke to him, blinded him, and instructed him to wait in Damascus for Ananias. When Ananias arrived, Paul's sight was restored. Then Ananias said to Paul:

> The God of our ancestors has chosen you to know his will and to see the Righteous One and hear Him speak. For you are to be His witness, telling everyone

what you have seen and heard. What are you waiting for? Get up and be baptized. Have your sins washed away by calling on the name of the Lord. (Acts 22:14-16 NLT)

Paul followed the instructions and returned to Jerusalem. But then in a vision he saw that he had to leave Jerusalem because the people would not believe him. He confessed that when Stephen, God's witness, was killed, he stood by and held the coats of those who stoned him. The Lord instructed Paul, *Go, for I will send you far away to the Gentiles!* (vs. 21).

When Paul said the word *Gentiles*, the hot-headed throng broke loose in fury. The captain of the Roman army took Paul inside the barracks and ordered that he be whipped. To stop this whipping, Paul revealed he was a Roman citizen, as it was against the law for them to beat a citizen. Then they released him from his chains. The following day he was taken before the Jewish Council.

On trial, Paul once again relayed his testimony. Disagreement arose in the counsel between the Pharisees and the Sadducees. When the conflict escalated, the Roman commander ordered the soldiers to remove Paul and escort him back to the safety of their military headquarters.

While Paul slept, the Lord appeared to him and said, *Be encouraged, Paul. Just as you have been a witness to me here in Jerusalem, you must preach the Good News in Rome as well* (Acts 23:11 NLT).

Paul had been arrested and tried, but had not received a verdict. The warnings he received from the Lord—confirmed by the prophecy of others—had come to pass. He was in jail in Jerusalem. While in jail, the Lord affirmed to him that he would go to Rome to preach the gospel. Though he received a word from the Lord, it did not come to pass right away.

Paul's nephew visited Paul in jail to inform him that the Jews plotted to kill him. The Roman soldiers were informed of this conspiracy, and they placed Paul under protective custody. They transferred Paul to Caesarea at night under the cover of darkness.

The commander wrote a letter to Governor Felix to explain how Paul was a Roman citizen and how the reasons for his arrest were uncertain, but they had something to do with Jewish customs. He stated that the accusations were not worthy of death, and Paul needed to be protected from the Jews.

After verifying Paul was a Roman citizen, Governor Felix agreed to hear his case when his accusers arrived from Jerusalem.

> Five days later Ananias, the high priest, arrived with some of the Jewish elders and the lawyer Tertullus, to present their case against Paul to the governor. When Paul was called in, Tertullus presented the charges against Paul. (Acts 24:1-2 NLT)

The charges are summed up as follows: Paul was a troublemaker. He stirred up riots among the Jews. He was a cult ringleader, and he desecrated the temple. The prosecutors in this case against Paul proclaimed they would have already judged him according to Jewish law had not the Roman commander Lysias removed him.

Then the governor gave Paul a chance to speak in his own defense. Paul denied arguing with anyone or stirring up riots. He admitted to being a believer and a follower of Christ, which they referred to as a cult. He went on to declare the allegations against him were false.

At this point, Governor Felix adjourned the court until he could hear the testimony of Lysias, after which he would make a decision on the case. But for some unknown reason, Lysias never appeared before the governor. Over a two-year period while Paul was imprisoned, Governor Felix called for him and listened to Paul's gospel message. But he did not really want to hear about Christ. The truth of the matter was he hoped Paul would bribe him.

After being incarcerated for two years, a new governor took over. Governor Festus arrived, and his first order of business was to meet with the chief priests in Jerusalem about Paul's case. The high counsel summoned the governor to transfer Paul back to Jerusalem to be tried in their court. But they secretly planned to assassinate Paul during the transfer.

> But Festus replied that Paul was at Caesarea and he himself would be returning there soon. So he said, "Those of you in authority can return with me. If Paul has done anything wrong, you can make your accusations." (Acts 25:4-5 NLT)

Several weeks later, court was held, and Paul faced his accusers. Once more, the unfounded accusations were presented. Paul denied the allegations of any crimes either against the Jews or against the Roman government.

After hearing the testimonies, Festus refused to make a decision. *Then Festus, wanting to please the Jews, asked him, "Are you willing to go to Jerusalem and stand trial before me there?"* (Acts 25:9 NLT).

Frustrated after being wrongfully imprisoned for two years, Paul made a sharp retort about Festus knowing he was not guilty, and that he did not have the right to turn him over to the Jews who wanted to kill him. Paul said, *I appeal to Caesar!* (Acts 25:11).

Paul petitioned the highest court of the land. This request set him on course to Rome, just as the Lord showed him in a dream two years prior. Over the next year, Paul survived a terrible storm on the Mediterranean Sea, a shipwreck on the island of Malta, and a poisonous snakebite before arriving in Rome.

Once in Rome, though imprisoned, Paul met with the Jews. He shared with them what happened to him in Jerusalem, but they had not received any news about Paul. He proceeded to share the gospel of Christ with the Jews. Some believed, and some did not. But for the next two years of Paul's imprisonment, he boldly proclaimed the kingdom of God.

Paul did not allow imprisonment to deter him from spreading the gospel. He knew he was called to preach about Jesus Christ in Rome, but I cannot imagine that he envisioned going to Rome as a prisoner.

Scholars vary on their opinions about Paul's obedience or disobedience in going to Jerusalem where he would be arrested. Did he bring this trouble on himself? Could it have been averted if he had listened to his friends? Or was it God's divine purpose for him?

The apostle Paul is accredited for writing thirteen letters of the New Testament. Some scholars say fourteen, as they give Paul credit for penning the book of Hebrews, though the author of Hebrews was not credited. Four of the thirteen epistles were written by Paul while he was confined in a Roman prison: Ephesians, Philippians, Colossians, and Philemon.

Known as the "prison epistles," the words penned by Paul from prison still witness to believers today. The Lord empowered Paul to change the lives of his time as well as many others throughout history to the present day and beyond with his writings.

The prison epistles are the most encouraging and hope-filled letters Paul wrote. The letters of hope contrast his physical condition. They show us how we can find joy in the midst of trials and find peace in our suffering. He shows how we can have spiritual strength to endure the trials that come into our lives with the power of the Holy Spirit.

From prison, Paul wrote that God *has blessed us with every spiritual blessing in the heavenly places in Christ* (Ephesians 1:3). What inspires me about the apostle Paul is that his faith never wavered in spite of being mocked, ridiculed, rejected, and imprisoned.

Paul set an example for believers who are prisoners and the families of the incarcerated. No matter what the circumstances are that led to the imprisonment, we can fulfill the calling of the Lord to witness God's goodness in trials and tribulations.

Prior to the circumstances that led to my son's arrest, he received a call from the Lord to serve as a missionary. Whether that means he will someday travel to foreign lands as we imagined—when that was prophesied to him years ago while on a short-term mission trip in Africa—is yet to be known.

But for the time being, while Stephen is serving his time to the state for the consequences of his choices, he is also serving the Lord where he is by sharing the gospel with those who otherwise may never hear the hope we have in Christ. His physical restraints have not stopped Stephen from seeking God's will for his life.

Though the appeal to the state court has not released Stephen, we continue to make an appeal to the courtroom of heaven.

PART II:

The Appeal Process

CHAPTER 8

Understanding the Courtroom of Heaven

People often ask me, "How do you know what to pray?"

As I have grown in my spiritual walk with the Lord, I have found in the Word of God that praying is something we must learn to do. In Luke 11 the disciples saw Jesus praying. When He finished, they said to Him, *Lord, teach us to pray, as John also taught his disciples* (Luke 11:1).

To teach means to "instill knowledge." So, if the disciples asked to be taught about prayer, shouldn't we also? In the introduction I mentioned that I studied prayer and taught others what I learned based on the Lord's Prayer found in Matthew 6 and Luke 11. This is where Jesus demonstrated for us how we should pray. Some theologians label it "The Model Prayer," while others call it "The Lord's Prayer." Whatever you choose to call it, Jesus taught his disciples—and us—how to pray.

This model shows us how to approach God as our Father with six distinct points that we include in our prayers. Those points are:

- We come to God our Father with reverence in praise and worship.
- We pray God's will be done.

- We present our petitions for our needs.

- We ask for forgiveness from God and forgive those who have hurt us.

- We ask for protection from the evil one.

- We close the prayer with more praise, giving God the glory.

In Luke 11:11-13 Jesus explained:

> If a son asks for bread from any father among you, will he give him a stone? Or if he asks for a fish, will he give him a serpent instead of a fish? Or if he asks for an egg, will he offer him a scorpion? If you then, being evil, know how to give good gifts to your children, how much more will your heavenly Father give the Holy Spirit to those who ask Him!

The point is that even if imperfect parents know how to give good things to their children, then our heavenly Father who is perfect desires to give us much more. All we have to do is ask.

In further study, I've learned there are several ways to pray. This information has been gleaned from various authors. My primary source for understanding these other ways to approach the Lord is through Robert Henderson's teachings on YouTube and in his books. In the appendix you will find a list of Henderson's books and other books that helped me gain insight on making appeals to the courtroom of heaven. I encourage you to pursue a more in-depth study on praying in this manner.

Since surrendering my life to Christ, I have always simply talked to God like we talk to one another. All throughout the day, when I have a question or just want to talk, I have conversations with the Lord. Sometimes I talk out loud. Other times it is just my thoughts. But I have learned to communicate with the Lord on a regular basis.

When I watched Henderson's teaching posted on YouTube, he pointed out that Scripture shows us one form of praying is like going to a friend when we have a need.

Jesus shared a parable after the Lord's Prayer in Luke:

> And He said to them, "Which of you shall have a friend, and go to him at midnight and say to him, 'Friend, lend me three loaves; for a friend of mine has come to me on his journey, and I have nothing to set before him' and he will answer from within and say, 'Do not trouble me; the door is now shut, and my children are with me in bed; I cannot rise and give to you'? I say to you, though he will not rise and give to him because he is his friend, yet because of his persistence he will rise and give him as many as he needs. So I say to you, ask, and it will be given to you; seek, and you will find; knock, and it will be opened to you. For everyone who asks receives, and he who seeks finds, and to him who knocks it will be opened." (Luke 11:5-10)

In this parable, Jesus likened prayer to an interaction between friends. We may go to God as we would with a friend, any time—even in the middle of the night.

The second dynamic of praying I learned from Henderson's teaching is that the parable of the persistent widow takes place in a judicial setting. This has been there all along, but I never looked at it from that perspective. Luke 18:1-8 says:

> Then He spoke a parable to them, that men always ought to pray and not lose heart, saying: "There was in a certain city a judge who did not fear God nor regard man. Now there was a widow in that city;

and she came to him, saying, 'Get justice for me from my adversary.' And he would not for a while; but afterward he said within himself, 'Though I do not fear God nor regard man, yet because this widow troubles me I will avenge her, lest by her continual coming she weary me.'"

Then the Lord said, "Hear what the unjust judge said. And shall God not avenge His own elect who cry out day and night to Him, though He bears long with them? I tell you that He will avenge them speedily. Nevertheless, when the Son of Man comes, will He really find faith on the earth?"

Jesus instructed us to always pray and never give up. Then He likens prayer to going to court. The example Jesus gave us in this parable is that if a persistent widow can get justice from a wicked, evil judge who did not fear God or have any concern for other people, we can trust and believe we will get righteous verdicts from the Righteous Judge.

This widow sought justice from her adversary. We all have an adversary who brings accusations against us before the Judge. Revelation 12:10 tells us that he accuses us *before our God day and night.* We all desire to find relief and find justice from the accusations and the burdens placed on us from the adversary.

In the first two forms of prayer, the Lord does not give us any indication when He will answer. In the parable of the persistent widow, we find that *He will avenge them speedily.* That gives us hope our prayers will be answered more quickly. Let's remember that God's speed is not our speed. We leave the timing up to Him for answering our petitions.

As prisoners and families of prisoners, you may have exhausted all your appeals with the government's system in this realm for your physical freedom. You may have filed all the writs of habeas corpus allowed. Or perhaps you have grown weary from filing the commutation or petitions for pardon paperwork. As believers in Christ, we have a right to appeal to the highest court, the courtroom of heaven, to seek a righteous verdict in the spiritual realm. Then who knows, the Lord may also release the physical prisoners like He did with King Manasseh. I have met formerly incarcerated people who were miraculously released from prison. I have also heard and read the testimonies of others. That shows me the Lord still releases prisoners from captivity as He wills. This fills me with hope, and I pray it stirs up your hope in the Lord too. How is that possible? Let me share some ways I have observed.

The Lord directs those who are in leadership over our nations. Proverbs 21:1 says, *The king's heart is in the hand of the Lord, like the rivers of water; He turns it wherever He wishes.* It doesn't matter whether the king is a Christian or not. When the Lord allowed the Israelites to be taken into captivity because they refused to repent and turn to Him, they were captured under King Nebuchadnezzar of Babylon. The Lord gave them a seventy-year sentence. When the time was served, the Lord directed the new reigning Babylonian King Cyrus to release the Hebrew people.

The U.S. elections are held every two to four years. This is an opportunity to place new leaders into office. For those who are eligible, we should go vote for those who are favorable to prison reform and new laws that help protect the rights of prisoners and their families.

On December 21, 2018, President Donald Trump signed the First Step Act into law. This was the first act of significant prison reform in the U.S. for over a decade. This new law for federal prisons gives inmates an opportunity to enroll in classes that will prepare them for a successful life on the outside, reducing recidivism. There are many other benefits such as earned-time credits, limiting restraints on pregnant prisoners, addressing unfair sentencing, and housing prisoners closer to home to name a few. Because of this new law, I know of families whose incarcerated loved ones were released earlier than expected. God uses our government leaders to set the captives free.[1]

As I visit with families and former offenders, other than the hardened and the unrepentant, I find there are three basic categories of prison situations: those who were rightfully convicted and sentenced justly, but truly repentant, those who were wrongfully convicted, and those who were rightfully convicted but received an unfair sentence.

You or your loved one may have been justifiably convicted of the crime but have since humbled yourself before the Lord God Almighty like King Manasseh did. Manasseh was considered the worst king of Israel. He was a known terrorist who slaughtered many people and should have received the death penalty. Yet because Manasseh humbled himself before the Lord, God released him and allowed him to return to his own land (2 Chronicles 33:11-13).

At my very first writers' conference in 2008, I met author Kent Whitaker. Hearing his testimony of unconditional love and forgiveness moved me to tears. His son, Bart Whitaker, received the death penalty after being convicted of plotting the murders of his family in 2003 in Houston, Texas. Bart hired two accomplices to carry out the murders in the family home. After returning home from a family dinner at a local restaurant, Bart's mother and brother were fatally shot upon entering the house. His father, Kent Whitaker, was the third to enter and received shots to the shoulder. Bart entered last and took a shot in the arm to divert suspicion.

After recalling the Scripture of God's promise to work all things out for good (Romans 8:28), Kent felt the grace of God come over him to forgive those responsible for the shooting, unaware it was his son who masterminded the attack. As the investigation unfolded, Kent learned the police determined his son, Bart, was the primary suspect in this case.

Kent felt strongly that the Lord spared his life for a reason. In his book, *Murder by Family*, Kent writes:

> It occurred to me that perhaps my purpose was to be God's agent of guidance and instruction for Bart. If he was innocent, I would be the anchor he relied on as he weathered the storms of suspicion; I wouldn't let him go through that horror alone. If he was guilty, I would be in a unique position to model God's unconditional forgiveness and love. I might be the person God would use to soften Bart's heart. And since I already had forgiven whoever was responsible, if Bart was guilty, he would be covered in pure forgiveness, granted before I ever thought it might apply to my son.[2]

For eleven years, this father petitioned the earthly courts and made his appeals to the courtroom of heaven to spare the life of his only remaining son. Just minutes prior to the scheduled execution on February 22, 2018, Texas Governor Greg Abbott commuted Bart Whitaker's death sentence to life without parole. Though he was not released from prison, now this father and son have the opportunity for contact visits, which was not allowed while Bart sat on death row. They give God the glory and testify of His goodness to others.

Perhaps you or your loved one was wrongfully convicted. In Genesis we read about Joseph, whose brothers sold him into slavery. While serving as a slave, his master's wife accused him of sexual misconduct. After these false allegations, Joseph was wrongfully convicted and imprisoned. Yet as a slave and a prisoner, the Lord was with Joseph and gave him success, prospering him in all his work.

The Lord used the poor choices of other people to position Joseph so he would be at the right place at the right time to be promoted to second-in-command of all of Egypt. The years of slavery and imprisonment prepared Joseph to be a leader to spare Egypt from suffering during a famine. Not only Egypt, but other countries and even his own family. Perhaps you or your loved one may be in the process of being positioned for a greater promotion.

You or your loved one may be guilty but received an unfair sentence. Too often as I share among prison family groups, I hear them compare types of convictions and the sentences rendered. Different judges or courts in different areas tend to sentence differently within the sentencing guidelines. First of all, we must be cautious about comparing. Theodore Roosevelt said, "Comparison is the thief of joy." More importantly, the Bible tells us it is unwise to compare ourselves with others. Second Corinthians 10:12 says, *For we dare not class ourselves or compare ourselves with those who commend themselves. But they, measuring themselves by themselves, and comparing themselves among themselves, are not wise.*

If you feel that you or your loved one received an unjust sentence, make an appeal to the courtroom of heaven, based on Leviticus 19:15: *Do not twist justice in legal matters by favoring the poor or being partial to the rich and powerful. Always judge people fairly* (NLT).

In his book *Unshackled*, Gene McGuire shares how at seventeen years old, he received life without parole for leaving the scene of a murder with his cousin who actually committed the homicide. After about ten years in prison, McGuire surrendered his life to the Lord while attending his first prison revival. Gene served the Lord inside prison by volunteering in ministry as much as possible. After his eleventh year in prison, he filed commutation papers for the first time. He was denied by the governor's board. Over the course of twenty-two years, he continued to file commutation papers, hoping to be released on parole. Each time McGuire received a denial letter. Though the rejection hurt, he returned to his cell and gave thanks to God based on First Thessalonians 5:16-18: *Rejoice always, pray without ceasing, in everything give thanks; for this is the will of God in Christ Jesus for you.*

With thirty years in prison and another denial letter, Gene wrote, "I walked back to my cell without talking to anyone. I collapsed to my knees next to my bunk and cried. Immediately, I heard the Lord say, 'Thank me.' And I did." Gene gave thanks to the Lord for His provision, for His protection, and for His providence. McGuire recalled many years of scenarios where he saw the Lord's guidance on his life within the prison walls.

Continuing to give thanks through his tears, hurt, and confusion, McGuire said, "And then I heard it—clear as day—God's voice: 'I will release you, Gene!' And He clarified, 'It's not going to be based on what you've done or who you know—I'm going to release you!'"[3]

Two months after the denial, Gene received a letter from an attorney who told him the government was investigating life-without-parole sentences given to minors as some laws had changed. Gene mustered up the courage to file commutation papers once again. He waited twenty months while the case was investigated. On April 3, 2012, McGuire was back in the courtroom. The judge declared "time served," and Gene McGuire was released.

For twenty-four years McGuire made an appeal to the courtroom of heaven by giving thanks to the Lord. Because he never gave up, he is now a free man sharing his testimony and giving glory to the Lord.

Throughout the Scriptures we see evidence that the Lord uses captivity as a form of temporal judgment, which was discussed in a previous chapter. Katie Souza of Expected End Ministries served five years of a thirteen-year federal sentence. In her *Captivity Series* books, she explains how God uses captivity to get people's attention and uses prison time to prepare them for their purpose. Katie says, "He has a bigger plan, an amazing plan where He wants to use captivity to totally give us our dreams, to give us our future. He loves us so much that He's got a plan for it, and it's way bigger than we thought it would be."[4]

Second Chronicles 7:14 says, *if My people who are called by My name will humble themselves, and pray and seek My face, and turn from their wicked ways, then I will hear from heaven, and will forgive their sin and heal their land.*

In this passage we find steps to freedom. First is the humbling of self before God and seeking Him. Jesus said, *But seek first the kingdom of God and His righteousness, and all these things shall be added to you* (Matthew 6:33). Our first priority is to seek the Lord through repentance. Repentance begins our relationship with the Lord, and repentance keeps us in right relationship with Him.

Second, we are to turn from the wicked ways. This means giving up the old lifestyle that is contrary to the Word of God. In Christ, we become a new creation (2 Corinthians 5:18). When we fall in love with our Lord, we have a desire to obey His ways. Jesus said, *If you love Me, keep my commandments* (John 14:15).

Joe Narvais received two life-without-parole sentences. While in prison, Joe asked Jesus to be his Advocate and to represent him in the courtroom of heaven. After turning from his wicked ways to follow Christ, Joe, like the persistent widow, continued to make his appeals. Joe wrote, "Thirteen years and eight months after I went to prison, I was paroled. But I had been free in my heart for years. I have been out now for over eleven years."

Just because you ask Jesus to be your Advocate and make good confessions, that will not get you out of prison. Joe explained, "You have to live a life of no compromise, totally sold out and surrendered to God. God gave us His very best in His Son Jesus. We need to give Jesus our very best. Our very best is a surrendered life with no compromise. You know what is right and wrong. Just do it."[5]

After humbling ourselves, seeking the Lord, and surrendering our bad lifestyle choices to follow the ways of the Lord, He will hear us, forgive us, and heal our land, which is God's promise of restoration.

The Lord desires to restore lives. A restored life may not look the way we want it to look, but God promises to give us more than we can think or imagine when we commit to living according to His will. Bart Whitaker was moved off death row where contact visits are prohibited. Now he is in general population where he is granted contact visits with his family. Gene McGuire sought parole, but when he surrendered to the Lord's will, God gave him time served. He's free to move about the country without reporting to the system. Joe Narvais had two life sentences, but he is living outside prison walls on parole. As of March 2018, Joe's reporting dates were changed from monthly to annually. That was more than he could have ever imagined.

If you have asked Jesus to be your Advocate, you are qualified to operate in and make your appeals in the courtroom of heaven. Most of us who have been walking with the Lord for some time have been praying in the courtroom of heaven, but simply have not recognized it as such.

We all have an adversary who brings accusations against us *before our God day and night* (Revelation 12:10). This shows me that not only will we stand in the courtroom of heaven in the eternal judgment, but our adversary calls us to court on a daily basis. The Enemy understands how to hinder our prayer petitions by filing his own petitions. To make effective appeals and ask for petitions, we must learn how to operate in the courtroom of heaven by silencing our accuser.

CHAPTER 9

Silencing the Accuser

We can enter into the courtroom of heaven at any time to bring our petitions before the Righteous Judge, but before presenting our petitions to Him, we must take appropriate steps to silence the accuser.

Ask Jesus to Be Your Advocate

First, in order to silence the accuser, we must ensure that Jesus is our Advocate. He is the only One qualified to represent us in the courtroom of heaven. As shared in Chapter 4, we must confess our sins, repent, and ask for forgiveness. Without this important step of placing our sins under the blood of Jesus, the prosecutor will use them against us. If you have not done this, go back to Chapter 4 to ask Jesus to be your Advocate.

Agree with the Adversary

Second, we must understand the role of Satan, our accuser. He is also known as our adversary, as discussed in Chapter 3. He opposes us and brings all our unconfessed sins against us to keep us from finding mercy in the courtroom of heaven. He will find ways to hinder us from filing our appeals to receive what Jesus Christ paid the price for us to receive—the blessings of God.

In Matthew 5:25 we are told, *Agree with your adversary quickly, while you are on the way with him, lest your adversary deliver you to the judge, the judge hand you over to the officer, and you be thrown into prison.* The Enemy sets traps to ensnare us in sin, which will place us in bondage. He will then use it against us as our accuser before God. But when we *agree with your adversary quickly*, meaning we confess and repent of our sins, we will have our cases thrown out of the courtroom of heaven.

A key reference to understand how to silence the accuser and to overcome him is found in Revelation 12:10-11:

> Then I heard a loud voice saying in heaven, "Now salvation, and strength, and the kingdom of our God, and the power of His Christ have come, for the accuser of our brethren, who accused them before our God day and night, has been cast down. And they overcame him by the blood of the Lamb and by the word of their testimony, and they did not love their lives to the death."

When we sin, the Enemy will take it to God anytime *day and night*. To silence our accuser, we must agree with him and repent for our sins. That puts them under the blood of the Lamb. I am so grateful the Lord made a way through Jesus Christ to set me free from the guilt and condemnation of the Enemy.

In understanding how to silence the accuser, we must recognize the most common tactics he uses against us. Gaining this insight is to expose him, not to condemn us. Romans 8:1 says, *So now the case is closed. There remains no accusing voice of condemnation against those who are joined in life-union with Jesus, the Anointed One* (TPT). This silences the accusing voice against us and closes our case.

Let's examine three primary strategies the accuser uses against us in the courtroom of heaven to hinder our appeals.

Willful and Known Sins

Willful sins are disobedience, which is refusing to obey the Word of God. We know what is wrong, but choose to live an immoral life anyway. Continued disobedience is rebellion against God and will lead us into bondage, making us a lawful captive. "A lawful captive is a person who is a prisoner legally. They have broken the law and have been taken to court and prosecuted, declared guilty, and have found themselves in captivity," Strauss explains in her book *From the Courtroom of Heaven to the Throne of Grace and Mercy.* [1]

First John 3:4 tells us, *Anyone who indulges in sin lives in moral anarchy, for the definition of sin is breaking God's law* (TPT). Breaking the law makes us a lawful captive. Willful disobedience not only places us in captivity, it allows the accuser to build his case against us. He stacks up a list of all our poor lifestyle choices.

Honestly confessing our sins and turning away from them will erase that evidence against us in the courtroom of heaven, thus silencing the accuser.

We must repent for all known sins, including the most common sins that many of us fall into on a daily basis such as worry, fear, and anxiety. I confess that for most of my life, I thought living with fear, worry, and anxiety was normal. While it may be normal for an unbeliever, for a born-again child of God, it is not. When we confess our sins and repent, the Lord is faithful to forgive us of our sins (1 John 1:9). When we confess and repent of sins, they are removed from our lives. Psalm 103:12 says, *As far as the east is from the west, so far has He removed our transgressions from us.*

When we receive Jesus, we also receive the gift of the Holy Spirit. Jesus promised us that when He ascended into heaven, He would send us a Helper, who is also known as the Spirit of Truth (John 14:16-17). Our Helper lives with us and guides us into all truth. He does that by giving us a feeling of remorse in our hearts so we know what sins are present and when we need to repent.

Second Corinthians 7:10 tells us, *For godly sorrow produces repentance leading to salvation, not to be regretted; but the sorrow of the world produces death.* There is a difference in being sorry we were caught in our sins and now face the consequences versus having sorrow that expresses remorse that we hurt God and others with our choices, regardless of the consequences.

When we feel remorse, we are faced with a choice. Oftentimes, that choice is made within a matter of seconds. We can choose to ignore it. When we ignore that nudge from the Holy Spirit, it begins the process of hardening our hearts.

Proverbs 28:13-14 says, *He who covers his sins will not prosper, but whoever confesses and forsakes them will have mercy. Happy is the man who is always reverent, but he who hardens his heart will fall into calamity.*

If we choose to ignore that nudge from the Holy Spirit to repent, our hearts will become hardened, and soon enough we will experience trouble in our lives. If we want to receive mercy in the courtroom of heaven, we must confess and forsake our sins to overcome the Enemy by the blood of the Lamb.

Salvation is not just being saved from eternal separation from God. In the Greek, the word is *soteria*, which means "deliverance and preservation."[2] That means our godly sorrow produces a repentance, which leads to our deliverance. We are delivered from the lawful captivity. And when we are set free from the bondage of sin, the case files the Enemy set up against us in the courtroom of heaven are closed.

> Thank God! Once you were slaves of sin, but now you wholeheartedly obey this teaching we have given you. Now you are free from your slavery to sin, and you have become slaves to righteous living. (Romans 6:17-18 NLT)

Release Others Through Forgiveness

Another way the Enemy hinders us in the courtroom of heaven is when we hold unforgiveness against others. He knows if he causes us to take an offense and stay offended, he has a legal right to oppose us before the Righteous Judge.

When Jesus taught the disciples to pray, He included a line in the prayer that says, *And forgive us our debts, as we forgive our debtors* (Matthew 6:12). After the *Amen,* He went on to explain, *For if you forgive men their trespasses, your heavenly Father will also forgive you. But if you do not forgive men their trespasses, neither will your Father forgive your trespasses* (vs.14-15).

That means if we want to be forgiven of our sins, we also must forgive others of their sins. Extending forgiveness does not mean we are weak. When we forgive, it makes us strong. Medical research shows forgiveness frees us from stress, anxiety, depression, and improves our physical well-being. Some physical health benefits to forgiveness include a stronger immune system, lower blood pressure, and improved heart health.

Living a lifestyle of forgiveness is part of living uprightly and eliminating the heavenly prosecutor's records of wrongs against us. Plus, forgiveness keeps us in right relationship with God and with others, frees us from demonic torment, releases us from bondage to others, releases God's divine healing power, and allows God to forgive us so that we will be granted our petitions in the courtroom of heaven.

Our human, fleshly nature desires to hold on to grudges. God's Word instructs us to let go of the hurt by forgiving those who offend us.

As I've visited with families of the incarcerated, I have met people who continue to hold on to offenses caused by the judicial system, the penal system, the media, and the general public. Offenses may be caused by one or more of the following:

- The one who was arrested.
- Those who weren't arrested but should have been.
- Other family members for what they should have or should not have done.
- The law enforcement officers for the way they handled the case.
- The prosecuting attorney who took a bad situation and made it much worse.
- The defense attorney who didn't fulfill his obligation.
- The judge who did not follow the law.
- The jury that made decisions on limited information presented in the trial.
- The probation/parole officers for how they work.
- The correction officers who excessively exert their powers.
- The warden who allowed mistreatment inside the prison.
- The parole board decisions.
- The media for how they reported the case.
- The public for expressing their opinions about it all.

If any or all of these persons have hurt or wronged you in any way directly or indirectly, I urge you to release them to the Lord by choosing to forgive them.

When you forgive another person for their wrongs against you, whether that wrong is legitimate (something that actually happened to you), perceived (something that did not really happen, but is how you see it in your mind's eye), or assumed (something that happened to someone you love, and you take on that offense as if it happened to you), you are not approving or excusing that behavior, forgetting what happened, or denying the pain. Nor does it mean you must reconcile with the person who hurt you.

When you forgive others, it keeps you in right relationship with God and allows God to forgive you and answer your petitions. If we choose not to forgive, it places us back into willful sin. Mark 11:25 says, *And whenever you stand praying, if you have anything against anyone, forgive him, that your Father in heaven may also forgive you your trespasses.*

When we refuse to forgive others (by choice), we are not forgiven of our own sins. That gives the Enemy legal right to our lives and stops our petitions from being answered from the throne room of God.

> Now whom you forgive anything, I also forgive. For if indeed I have forgiven anything, I have forgiven that one for your sakes in the presence of Christ, lest Satan should take advantage of us; for we are not ignorant of his devices. (2 Corinthians 2:10-11)

The apostle Paul made it clear to the Corinthians that he forgave those they had forgiven. Otherwise, Satan would have been able to take advantage of them. We also must forgive so we do not give Satan a legal right to operate in our lives.

When choosing forgiveness, we need to forgive that person for *each* specific offense against us. Yes, this may take some time, especially if we have been in relationship with someone for a long time. Allow the Holy Spirit, your Helper, to show you what areas you need to forgive and when. All of this is *not* going to happen at once, but each time you come back to make your appeals to the courtroom of heaven, it is best to ask if there is anyone you need to forgive and the specific offense. Let Him guide you in this process.

Not only do we need to forgive others, we must forgive ourselves. Too often, we may knowingly or unknowingly hold grudges against ourselves. When we feel angry for something we messed up on, or we feel guilt for anything we should or should not have done, that may be a sign we are holding unforgiveness against ourselves. We must repent for the wrong behavior and forgive.

Some hurts, wounds, and offenses in our lives are very deep. The Lord Jesus came to heal the brokenhearted, and only by His grace are those traumas healed. *He heals the brokenhearted and binds up their wounds* (Psalm 147:3). And when Jesus picked up the scroll and read from the prophet Isaiah, He said that the Scripture was fulfilled that day:

> The Spirit of the LORD IS UPON ME, because He has anointed Me to preach the gospel to the poor; He has sent Me to heal the brokenhearted, to proclaim liberty to the captives and recovery of sight to the blind, to set at liberty those who are oppressed. (Luke 4:18)

Part of what Jesus completed through His life, death, and resurrection was the healing of all the broken places in our hearts.

Because of the offenses against us that have wounded our hearts (our emotions), we seal the forgiveness prayer by asking the Lord to heal all the broken places in our heart. Sometimes the broken places take time to heal just like a broken bone. Other times, it may be only a day or perhaps even an instant. Once our brokenness is healed by Jesus, we will no longer feel the emotional pain associated with the memory. We may even completely forget the incident ever happened. What a blessing it is to become more like the Father who does not remember our transgressions against Him.

Repentance of the Sins of Forefathers

The accuser is relentless and will continue to search for reasons to hinder us from receiving a righteous verdict from the Just Judge. Another hindrance that we need to silence from the accuser may be the sins of our forefathers. Once again, we must agree with the adversary and pray for forgiveness of the sins of our forefathers. We see many scriptural examples of prayers repenting for those in the generations before us.

While in captivity in Babylon, Nehemiah prayed when he felt the desire to go rebuild the torn-down wall in Jerusalem. *Both my father's house and I have sinned* (Nehemiah 1:7). Later, after the king released Nehemiah to go back to his homeland and rebuild the walls of Jerusalem, he gathered the people of Israel together and prayed. *And they stood and confessed their sins and the iniquities of their fathers* (Nehemiah 9:2).

Daniel prayed a prayer of repentance for those before him prior to lifting up his petitions:

> O Lord, to us belongs shame of face, to our kings, our princes, and our fathers, because we have sinned against You. To the Lord our God belongs mercy and forgiveness, though we have rebelled against Him. We have not obeyed the voice of the Lord our God, to walk in His laws, which He set before us by His servants the prophets. Yes, all Israel has transgressed Your law and has departed so as not to obey Your voice; therefore, the curse and the oath written in the Law of Moses the servant of God have been poured out on us, because we have sinned against Him. (Daniel 9:8-11)

Many times, the things we label as being inherited from our parents or grandparents may be part of what the Bible calls a curse. Exodus 20:5 states that the Lord will visit the iniquity of the fathers down to the third and fourth generation.

But we tend to laugh them off, make excuses for certain behaviors, or justify what the Bible calls a curse. What we say to one another at family gatherings may be a sign there is a generational curse operating in our lives. Some examples are:

- You have your grandfather's temper.

- No one in our family has ever been able to save money for emergencies.

- She inherited the family trait to take charge and control others.

Other signs of generational curses operating in our lives are repeated patterns of behaviors through the family ancestors such as divorce, inherited illnesses, addictions, financial issues, accidents, and anger. Those are just a few examples of an ancestral curse.

In his book *Shadowboxing,* Dr. Henry Malone wrote, "Ancestral curses are one of the major ways that Satan gains legal ground into our lives. These curses can be defined as a 'strong constant propensity within us.'"[3]

Though we may be drawn to behave in the same manner as our forefathers, the Lord made a way for us to be set free from those inherited behaviors. That's good news.

Once we identify those ancestral curses that have drawn us away from the Lord or enticed us to be drawn away from Him, we repent by placing them under the blood of Jesus. This act of repenting for the sins of our forefathers stops the Enemy's legal right to operate in our lives. *Christ has redeemed us from the curse of the law, having become a curse for us (for it is written, "Cursed is everyone who hangs on a tree")* (Galatians 3:13).

When we place those known ancestral sins under the blood of Jesus, who redeemed us from the curse of the law, the Enemy no longer has legal right to use those sins against us in the courtroom of heaven. Otherwise, he will use that strategy against us to hinder our petitions and keep our prayers from being answered.

Each time we enter the courtroom of heaven, we have our Advocate. It is through Him we silence the accuser.

We can identify accusations the Enemy is presenting by our thoughts and negative emotions. If we think of a person or incident that causes us to feel a negative emotion such as anger, frustration, or sadness, that may be an indication the accuser is presenting a case before the Righteous Judge. As soon as we recognize it, we can pray a prayer of repentance and forgiveness (found in the next chapter) and place it under the blood of Jesus as quickly as possible.

Our willingness to repent of all that the accuser brings before the court is necessary for us to operate in the courts of heaven. Otherwise, any petitions brought before the court will be hindered.

There is much more the Enemy uses against us than what is listed in this chapter. Understanding these basics will allow the Righteous Judge to reverse the verdicts against us due to known sins, unforgiveness, and the sins of the forefathers. As we seek the Lord, He leads us to the information we need as we mature in Him.

With this understanding of the most common hindrances Satan uses against us, we silence the accuser and are prepared to confidently take our petitions into the courtroom of heaven.

Let us therefore come boldly to the throne of grace, that we may obtain mercy and find grace to help in time of need (Hebrews 4:16).

CHAPTER 10

Preparing to Petition the Courtroom of Heaven

To appeal to the courtroom of heaven through prayer we must first prepare ourselves. None of us would show up to an earthly court appearance without preparation. After understanding how to silence the accuser, we must now prepare ourselves to present petitions to the courtroom of heaven.

Why do we need to present these petitions? We must understand that praying for ourselves and for others is an act of obedience. God commands us to pray. Here is a list of Scriptures that instruct us to pray:

- *Pray for those who persecute you.* (Matthew 5:44 NLT)

- *When you pray ...* (Matthew 6:5 NLT)

- *Pray like this ...* (Matthew 6:9 NLT)

- *Rejoice in our confident hope. Be patient in trouble, and keep on praying.* (Romans 12:12 NLT)

- *Pray in the Spirit at all times and on every occasion. Stay alert and be persistent in your prayers for all believers everywhere.* (Ephesians 6:18 NLT)

- *Don't worry about anything; instead, pray about everything. Tell God what you need, and thank him for all he has done.* (Philippians 4:6 NLT)

- *Devote yourselves to prayer with an alert mind and a thankful heart.* (Colossians 4:2 NLT)

- *Never stop praying.* (1 Thessalonians 5:17 NLT)

- *I urge you, first of all, to pray for all people. Ask God to help them; intercede on their behalf, and give thanks for them.* (1 Timothy 2:1 NLT)

Because we are children of God, we are also *heirs of God and joint heirs with Christ* (Romans 8:17). Our rebirth in Christ grants us the privilege to receive all that Christ receives because of what He did for us on the cross. Second Peter 1:2-4 tells us we have been given these promises:

> Grace and peace be multiplied to you in the knowledge of God and of Jesus our Lord, as His divine power has given to us all things that pertain to life and godliness, through the knowledge of Him who called us by glory and virtue, by which have been given to us exceedingly great and precious promises, that through these you may be partakers of the divine nature, having escaped the corruption that is in the world through lust.

What an excellent benefit as a child of God. I am certain after understanding this you feel the way I do and want to receive the benefit of all God's precious promises. To receive them, we are to ask for them. Matthew 7:7 says, *Ask, and the gift is yours. Seek, and you'll discover. Knock, and the door will be opened for you* (TPT).

How many times have we missed out on something because we didn't know what to ask for? That's why it is so vital to know the Word, because it contains His promises, the benefits He has for us. We ask, seek, and knock based on God's Word. That's the basis of our petitions in the courtroom of heaven.

When we pray God's Word, it does what He sent it to do. Isaiah 55:11 says, *So shall My Word be that goes forth from My mouth. It shall not return to Me void, but it shall accomplish what I please, and it shall prosper in the thing for which I sent it.*

God answers our petitions when we ask according to His will. How do we know what God's will is? God's Word is His will. Matthew 6:10 says, *Your kingdom come. Your will be done on earth as it is in heaven.* We do not have to wait until heaven to receive everything that is rightfully ours. As children of God, we can petition the courtroom of heaven to receive kingdom benefits while living on earth.

When we make our petitions with God's Word, we are praying with confidence that God will do what He says He will do. *Now this is the confidence we have in Him, that if we ask anything according to His will, He hears us. And if we know that He hears us, whatever we ask, we know that we have the petitions that we have asked of Him* (1 John 5:14-15).

Based on Revelation 12:11, we overcome, first *by the blood of the Lamb.* That's placing our sins under the blood of Jesus through repentance. Second, we overcome *by the word of their* (our) *testimony.* We need to present testimonies on our behalf in the courtroom. The testimony is the testimony of Jesus, who is the Word. *In the beginning was the Word, and the Word was with God, and the Word was God* (John 1:1).

When we petition the Righteous Judge based on the Word of God, we can have confidence that God will do what He says He will do, and we will overcome the accuser with the Word of His testimony.

Presenting a Petition for Another

In her book, *From the Courtroom of Heaven: Prayers & Petitions*, Jeanette Strauss explains how we may become an ambassador of reconciliation for another person or situation.

Second Corinthians 5:20-21 says:

> So we are Christ's ambassadors; God is making his appeal through us. We speak for Christ when we plead, "Come back to God!" For God made Christ, who never sinned, to be the offering for our sin, so that we could be made right with God through Christ (NLT).

The Lord desires for us to make an appeal to the courtroom of heaven on the behalf of others whom we love to *come back to God.* We do so as an ambassador of reconciliation, which is also known as an intercessor. An intercessor is one who prays on behalf of another or stands in the gap for them. That phrase comes from Ezekiel 22:30:

> I looked for someone who might rebuild the wall of righteousness that guards the land. I searched for someone to stand in the gap in the wall so I wouldn't have to destroy the land, but I found no one (NLT).

In that passage, Ezekiel searched for someone who saw the plight of Jerusalem so they could pray for the city. But he found no one. There are times others do not know they need prayer, or they are not able to pray for themselves due to the nature of their circumstances.

As believers, we are called to pray for one another. Parents are to pray for their children. Spouses are to pray for one another. Brothers and sisters in the body of Christ are to lift each other up in prayer.

We see the wayward lifestyles of loved ones and desire for them to turn their hearts to the Lord. To silence the accuser, we must implement the strategies revealed in the previous chapter and repent on their behalf. Strauss explains:

> If the person is not present to repent on behalf of their own sin, then you can stand in the gap on behalf of sin they are committing against the Lord and His Word. This isn't to say we can repent for the person. We are asking for a temporary reprieve for the sin they are committing against the Lord, so that He will remove the veil from their eyes and they will be able to see the truth and come to repentance.[1]

Or we may be praying for a person who has a close relationship with the Lord, yet they are not aware of accusations the Enemy has against them in the courtroom of heaven. By seeking the Lord, the Holy Spirit will show us where to seek a temporary reprieve and repent on their behalf. Then He will guide us in how to petition for them.

We all need intercessors in our lives. I am grateful to receive calls from time to time from others who said they have prayed for me. Sometimes I'm able to share testimony of how the Lord answered their prayers. Other times, I believe by faith that the Lord averted something I may never know about until I reach heaven. Praying for others makes a significant difference, even if we do not see the outward results.

All the petitions that follow are based on Scriptures, and you will find the references used in the prayers noted in the Prepare Your Case section related to that topic. I encourage you to meditate on the Scriptures prior to raising your petitions as it is important to understand God's Word in order to feel confident when you pray. The Lord may show you more Scriptures as you seek Him. I encourage you to write those down, include them in the list, and add them to your prayers.

In the Presenting Your Petition section, the Scriptures are reworded as prayers. Pray the Scriptures out loud before the Lord. Speaking the Word builds our faith, because we hear it. *So faith comes from hearing, that is, hearing the Good News about Christ* (Romans 10:17 NLT).

When we pray in faith, we believe God will honor His Word. Romans 4:17 tells us to call *those things which do not exist as though they did.* This is how God spoke the world into existence. Using our faith and praying according to God's Word by speaking it out loud will give us the confidence we need to appeal to the courtroom of heaven for ourselves and others.

My desire is for the incarcerated to pray for their families on the outside and for all the families on the outside to pray for their imprisoned loved ones. I want to reiterate that prayer makes a huge difference in our lives. The following petitions are guidelines for you to follow to petition the courtroom of heaven for yourself. There are other petitions to pray as an ambassador of reconciliation on the behalf of others.

In a courtroom setting, we always show respect. Otherwise, we would be asked to leave or held in contempt of court. When we enter into the courtroom of heaven, we must enter with humility, showing reverence and honor to the Lord. *Enter into His gates with thanksgiving and into His courts with praise. Be thankful to Him, and bless His name* (Psalm 100:4).

The prayer petitions in this book begin with Scriptures that lift up praise to the Lord and offer Him thanks. We seal our requests by asking for our petitions in the name of Jesus. Jesus said, *And whatever you ask in My name, that I will do, that the Father may be glorified in the Son. If you ask anything in My name, I will do it* (John 14:13-14). He also said in John 16:24,

Until now you have asked nothing in My name. Ask, and you will receive, that your joy may be full. When we make our petitions to the Father, the Righteous Judge of all, in the name of Jesus, we will receive so the Son may be glorified, and our joy will be full. What a glorious promise from the Lord above.

———————

The following prayers in this chapter only need to be prayed at the beginning of our prayer session. Then we may proceed to the next section to lift our petitions into the courtroom of heaven for ourselves and our loved ones.

Remember, the process below is not a formula but merely a prayer strategy. These guidelines teach us how to effectively appeal to the courtroom of heaven. According to the Word, we are to seek the Lord, repent for our sins, forgive others, and then He will hear our prayers. As we grow in our relationship with the Lord, the Holy Spirit guides us in how and when to pray.

There may be times we start to raise petitions to the Lord, and the Holy Spirit will bring back to our remembrance something from our past that needs to put under the blood through repentance or forgiveness. That is an indication the accuser is presenting an accusation against us before the Righteous Judge.

Whenever that happens, it is important for us to pray the prayer of repentance for ourselves or forgiveness/ repentance for the sins of our forefathers as the Holy Spirit shows us. Otherwise, the Enemy has legal right to hinder our petitions. Once the issue is under the blood, the accuser is then silenced by the blood of the Lamb, and we may continue to lift our petitions with confidence that the Lord will grant our request.

Prayer of Repentance

Your Honor, the Just and Righteous God, I bless Your holy name, the name above all names. Lord, I thank You that You promise if I confess my sins, You are faithful and will forgive me of my sins and cleanse me from all unrighteousness.

Today, I seek to enter Your presence in the courtroom of heaven and make my appeal. I come to You seeking forgiveness of all my sins. I pray as David did in Psalm 51: *Have mercy upon me, O God, according to Your loving kindness; according to the multitude of Your tender mercies, blot out my transgressions. Wash me thoroughly from my iniquity, and cleanse me from my sin. For I acknowledge my transgressions, and my sin is always before me. Against You, You only, have I sinned, and done this evil in Your sight— that You may be found just when You speak, and blameless when You judge. Behold, I was brought forth in iniquity, and in sin my mother conceived me. Behold, You desire truth in the inward parts, and in the hidden part You will make me know wisdom. Purge me with hyssop, and I shall be clean; wash me, and I shall be whiter than snow. Make me hear joy and gladness, that the bones You have broken may rejoice. Hide Your face from my sins, and blot out my iniquities. Create in me a clean heart, O God, and renew a steadfast spirit within me. Do not cast me from Your presence, and do not take Your Holy Spirit from me. Restore to me the joy of Your salvation, and uphold me by Your generous Spirit.*

Lord, I desire to confess and repent of all my sins and forsake them, not covering them up. I repent of _____ (begin listing any sins that come to mind as the

Holy Spirit prompts you. Be as specific as possible—fear, worry, doubt, anger, hatred, self-hatred, jealousy, coveting, idolatry, judgment, criticism, lying, etc.).

In Jesus, I have redemption through His blood and the forgiveness of my trespasses according to the riches of His grace. You are able to keep me from stumbling and to present me faultless before the presence of Your glory with exceeding joy. Lord, You blot out my transgressions for Your own sake and will not remember my sins. You tell me to put You in remembrance and to state my case so I may be acquitted. In Christ, I am a new creation. The old has gone. You have reconciled me to Yourself through Jesus Christ. For You made Christ, who knew no sin, to be sin for me, that I could become the righteousness of God in Christ.

Your Word says that a reverent person is happy. I receive Your joy today as I cleanse myself in Your presence. Before, I was a slave to sin, but now I desire to obey You with all my heart and all the teachings in Your Word so I may be set free from the bondage to sin and be a bondservant to right living.
In Jesus' name, Amen.

Scripture references: 1 John 1:9; Psalm 32:5; Ephesians 1:7; Jude 1:24; Isaiah 43:25-26; 2 Corinthians 5:18-19; 2 Corinthians 5:21

Prayer to Forgive

Lord, Your Word says that if I have anything against anyone, I am to forgive him just as You forgive me. I desire to be obedient to Your Word. So, Father, in the name of Jesus Christ, as an act of my will, I choose to forgive

_____ for _____. (Name all persons who come to your thoughts and each specific offense.) I also forgive myself for self-condemnation, self-guilt, self-rejection, and self-hatred related to _____ (name the incident). You forgive me; therefore, I forgive myself. I ask for forgiveness for holding anything against them and against myself. I ask You, Lord, to heal my broken heart and bind up all my wounds. This I pray in Jesus' name, Amen.

Scripture References: Mark 11:25; Psalm 147:3

Prayer of Repentance for Sins of Forefathers

Lord, I thank You that Christ has redeemed me from the curse of the law, as He became a curse for me when He hung on the cross. I repent for the sins and iniquities of my forefathers, because you say You are a jealous God and will visit the iniquity of the fathers down to the third and fourth generation.

Lord, I bring my bloodline to You through my parents (name them), their parents (name your grandparents), and all those back through generations since Adam and Eve before You. I repent for _____. (Be specific of known sins of your forefathers, and ask the Holy Spirit to reveal to you any unknown sins the Enemy may use against you in the courtroom of heaven. Examples may be rebellion, pride, addictions, divorce, promiscuity, ungodly alliances, occult practices, hatred, family feuds, anger, and unkind words.)

Lord, Your Word says that a curse without a cause cannot come. I ask that the sins of my past generations be placed under the blood of Jesus so the Enemy has no cause to send the curse in the spirit realm or the physical realm. Your Word says we have a mediator of a new covenant between You and me, the sprinkled blood of Jesus that speaks of forgiveness. Thank You for covering all these past sins with the blood that speaks for me.

Thank You for cancelling all the charges against me and my bloodline by nailing them to the cross. Thank You that You are my God, keeping a covenant of mercy for a thousand generations with those who love You and keep Your commandments. I give you praise because you have blessed us with every spiritual blessing because we are united with Christ Jesus. I receive and accept Your forgiveness for my forefathers in Jesus' name, Amen.

Scripture references: Galatians 3:13; Exodus 20:5; Proverbs 26:2; Hebrews 12:24; Colossians 2:14; Deuteronomy 7:9; Ephesians 1:3

Prayer as an Ambassador of Reconciliation

Pray this prayer prior to choosing any of the Present a Petition for Another prayers in the next section:

Your Honor, I come before You today to petition on the behalf of _____ (name the person or persons you are praying for). I ask for a temporary reprieve from the legal accusations by the Enemy by asking for Your forgiveness of _____'s sins and that You wash him/ her with the blood of Jesus. I pray You remove the veil from _____'s eyes to see the truth and come to a place of godly sorrow that leads to repentance. May _____ experience the freedom and abundance of life that Christ came to give. in Jesus' name, Amen.

PART III:

Petitions for the Courtroom of Heaven

Freedom from Addictions

Prepare Yourself

Be sure you have prayed through the Preparing to Petition the Courtroom of Heaven prayers in chapter ten. Include the Ambassador of Reconciliation prayer if you will be petitioning on behalf of others.

Prepare Your Case

Look up and meditate on these Scripture references: 1 Chronicles 16:8; Proverbs 20:1; James 4:7; 1 Peter 2:11; Galatians 5:16; Matthew 6:13; 1 Corinthians 10:13; Psalm 50:15; Titus 2:12; Matthew 26:41; Philippians 4:16; 2 Samuel 22:4

Add any additional Scriptures the Lord shows you.

Present a Petition for Yourself

Lord, I give thanks to You and call upon Your name. I will make known Your deeds among the people. Your Word says that wine is a mocker, strong drink leads to brawls, and those who succumb to it become fools. Lord, I desire to submit myself to You and resist the Devil so he will flee from me. I choose to abstain from the lust of the flesh that wars against my soul. I will put on the Lord Jesus Christ who helps me to live as I should. I will not make any provision for my flesh so that I no longer enjoy evil. I now walk in the Spirit and no longer fulfill the desires of the evil nature. Do not let me fall into temptation, but keep me safe from the evil one. Lord, You are faithful and will not allow me to be tempted any more than I can stand. When I am tempted, You show me a way out so I can endure it. I will call upon You in my day of trouble, and You will deliver me. I say no to ungodliness and worldly passions and live a self-controlled, upright, and godly life in this present age. I will watch and pray so that I will not fall into temptation, for the spirit is willing, but the flesh is weak. I can do all things through Christ who strengthens me. I call upon the Lord and praise Him for then I am saved from my enemies. This I pray in Jesus' name, Amen.

Present a Petition for Another

Lord, I give thanks to You and call upon Your name. I will tell others about your goodness. Your Word says wine is a mocker, strong drink leads to arguments, and those who give in to it become fools. Lord, may _____ submit his/her life to You and resist the Devil so he will flee. Thank you that _____ chooses to abstain from the lust of the flesh that wars against the soul. _____ will put on the Lord Jesus Christ and live according to your Word. _____ will not make any provision for the flesh and no longer enjoys evil. _____ now walks in the Spirit and no longer fulfills the desires of the evil nature. Keep _____ from the evil one, and do not let _____ fall into temptation. Lord, You are faithful and will not allow _____ to be tempted any more than he/she can stand. When tempted, You will help _____ endure, and provide a way out. _____will call upon You in the day of trouble and You will deliver. Thank you that _____ says no to ungodliness and worldly passions and lives a self-controlled, upright, and godly life in this present age. _____ will watch and pray and not fall into temptation, for the spirit is willing, but the flesh is weak. _____ can do all things through Christ who gives us strength. _____ is saved from his/her enemies by calling upon Your name and praising You. This I pray in Jesus' name, Amen.

Blessing Others

Prepare Yourself

Be sure you have prayed through the Preparing to Petition the Courtroom of Heaven prayers in chapter ten. Include the Ambassador of Reconciliation prayer if you will be petitioning on behalf of others.

Prepare Your Case

Look up and meditate on these Scripture references: Luke 6:28; Matthew 5:44; Luke 6:35; 1 Peter 3:9; Romans 12:18-21; 2 Corinthians 5:17

Add any additional Scriptures the Lord shows you.

Present a Petition for Yourself

Lord, I pray a blessing for those who have cursed me and for those who have mistreated me. Your Word says to love my enemies and to pray for those who persecute me. I am to love them and do good to them. To lend to them and expect nothing in return. As I do, You promise a great reward from heaven.

Lord, I desire to do all I can to live at peace with everyone. I will not take revenge, but will leave that to Your righteous anger. For Your Word says You will take revenge and pay them back. When my enemies are hungry, I will feed them. When they are thirsty, I will give them a drink. By doing this, I am heaping burning coals on their heads. I will not allow evil to conquer me, but I will conquer evil by doing good. I will not repay evil with evil or insult with insult, but will repay evil with a blessing, because that is what I am called to do so that I may inherit a blessing.

Lord, You know who I am now, a new creation in Christ Jesus. The old is gone. As a beloved child, I desire to be an imitator of God. Therefore, I bless and not curse. This I pray in Jesus' name, Amen.

Present a Petition for Another

Lord, I pray a blessing for those who have cursed or mistreated _____. You say in Your Word to love our enemies and to pray for those who persecute us. We are to love them and do good to them. To lend to them and expect nothing in return. As _____ does that, You promise a great reward from heaven.

I pray that _____ desires to live at peace with everyone. _____ will not take revenge, but will leave that to Your righteous anger. For Your Word says You will take revenge and pay them back. When his/her enemies are hungry, _____ will feed them. When they are thirsty, _____ will give them a drink. By doing this, burning coals are heaped upon the heads of our enemies. _____ will not be conquered with evil but will conquer evil by doing good. _____ will not repay evil with evil or insult with insult, but will repay evil with a blessing, because that is what we are called to do in order to inherit a blessing.

Lord, You know _____ is now a new creation in Christ Jesus. The old is gone. As a beloved child, _____ desires to be an imitator of God. Therefore, _____ blesses and does not curse. This I pray in Jesus' name, Amen.

Healing for the Brokenhearted

Prepare Yourself

Be sure you have prayed through the Preparing to Petition the Courtroom of Heaven prayers in chapter ten. Include the Ambassador of Reconciliation prayer if you will be petitioning on behalf of others.

Prepare Your Case

Look up and meditate on these Scripture references: Isaiah 41:13; Psalm 34:18; Psalm 38:17; Matthew 11:28-30; Psalm 73:26; Psalm 147:3; Psalm 32:7

Add any additional Scriptures the Lord shows you.

Present a Petition for Yourself

You are the Lord God who holds my right hand, saying to me, *Fear not for I will help you.* You are close to the brokenhearted and rescue those whose spirits are crushed. I am about ready to collapse as I deal with this pain. Jesus, You said to come to You when I am weary and when I am carrying heavy burdens so that You can give me rest. You said I am to take Your yoke upon me and let You teach me, for You are humble and gentle at heart. Then I will find rest for my soul, for Your yoke is easy, and the burden You give me is light. Though my health may fail and my spirit grow weak, You, my God, remain the strength of my heart. You are forever mine. You heal my broken heart and bind up my wounds. *You are my hiding place; you protect me from trouble. You surround me with songs of victory.* This I pray in Jesus' name, Amen.

Present a Petition for Another

You are the Lord God who holds our right hand, saying, *Fear not for I will help you.* You are close to _____, who is brokenhearted. You will rescue _____, whose spirit is crushed, ready to collapse with this pain. Jesus, You said for us to come to You when weary and carrying heavy burdens, and You will give us rest. You said for _____ to take on Your yoke, for You are humble and gentle at heart. Your yoke is easy, and the burden You give is light. Then _____ will find rest for the soul. Though _____'s health may fail, and his/her spirit may grow weak, You are the God who remains the strength of our heart. You are forever ours. Lord, You heal _____'s broken heart and bind up every wound. You are _____'s hiding place, and will protect from trouble. You surround each of us with songs of victory. This I pray in Jesus' name, Amen.

Freedom from Depression

Prepare Yourself

Be sure you have prayed through the Preparing to Petition the Courtroom of Heaven prayers in chapter ten. Include the Ambassador of Reconciliation prayer if you will be petitioning on behalf of others.

Prepare Your Case

Look up and meditate on these Scripture references: Isaiah 61:1-3; Psalm 119:28; Psalm 119:105; Psalm 112:4; Psalm 26:3; John 14:1; Romans 12:2; 1 Corinthians 2:16; Psalm 18:2; Nehemiah 8:10; Psalm 62:5-6

Add any additional Scriptures the Lord shows you.

Present a Petition for Yourself

Jesus came to comfort the brokenhearted and to tell those who mourn that the Lord's favor has come. You give me beauty for ashes, the oil of joy for mourning, and a garment of praise for the spirit of heaviness, so that I may be called a tree of righteousness, the planting of the Lord so that You may be glorified. Though my heart is heavy, I am encouraged. For Your Word is a lamp to guide my feet and a light for my path. Your light shines in the darkness for the godly. You keep me in perfect peace as I trust in and fix my thoughts on You. I will not let my heart be troubled, for I trust in You. I allow You, my Lord, to transform my being by changing the way I think so I will understand what

Your good and pleasing and perfect will is for me. You have given me the mind of Christ. I find protection in the Lord who is my rock, my fortress, and my Savior. You are my shield and my place of safety. I will not be dejected or sad, for the joy of the Lord is my strength. Your Word tells me to wait quietly, because my hope is in You alone. You are my rock, my salvation, and my fortress. I will not be shaken. This I pray in Jesus' name, Amen.

Present a Petition for Another

Jesus came to comfort the brokenhearted and to tell those who mourn that the Lord's favor has come. You give _____ beauty for ashes, the oil of joy for mourning, and a garment of praise for the spirit of heaviness, so that _____ may be called a tree of righteousness, the planting of the Lord so that You may be glorified. Though _____'s heart is heavy, it is encouraged. For Your Word is a lamp to guide our feet and light our path. Your light shines in the darkness for the godly. I thank you that you keep _____ in perfect peace, as _____ trusts in and fixes his/her thoughts on You. You will not let _____'s heart be troubled. Transform _____ by changing the way he/she thinks. Reveal Your good and pleasing and perfect will. You have given _____ the mind of Christ. May _____ find protection in the Lord, our rock, our fortress, and our Savior. You, Lord, are _____'s shield and place of safety. _____ shall not be dejected or sad for the joy of the Lord is his/her strength. I believe _____ will wait quietly before You and will not be shaken. This I pray in Jesus' name, Amen.

Faith Not Fail

Prepare Yourself

Be sure you have prayed through the Preparing to Petition the Courtroom of Heaven prayers in chapter ten. Include the Ambassador of Reconciliation prayer if you will be petitioning on behalf of others.

Prepare Your Case

Look up and meditate on these Scripture references: Psalm 117:2; Romans 12:3; Hebrews 11:1; Hebrews 11:6; Mark 11:24; Mark 17:20; James 1:6-8; Galatians 6:9-10; Ephesians 6:16; 1 Timothy 1:12

Add any additional Scriptures the Lord shows you.

Present a Petition for Yourself

Your love for me is great, and Your faithfulness endures forever, so I praise You, Lord. By grace You have given to me a measure of faith, the substance of things hoped for and the evidence of things not seen. I know without faith it is impossible to please You, so I come to You in faith knowing You reward me for seeking You. Jesus, You said when I pray and ask for something, I am to believe, then I will receive. Lord, I diligently seek You and believe You will answer my prayers concerning (list your concerns here). Some of these issues are as high as a mountain, so as Jesus instructed me, I say to that mountain to move out of the way. Lord, nothing is impossible for You. I ask this in faith and with no doubt. I will not grow weary in doing good, for in due season I will reap if I do not give up. Above all, I take up the shield of faith for which I am able to quench all the fiery darts of the wicked one. And I thank Christ Jesus my Lord who has enabled me, because He counts me faithful. I believe Your promises and I sing Your praise. In Jesus' name I pray, Amen.

Present a Petition for Another

Your love for us is great, and Your faithfulness endures forever, so I thank you that _____ will praise Your name. By grace You have given _____ a measure of faith, which is the substance of things hoped for and the evidence of things not seen. Knowing that without faith it is impossible to please You, _____ goes to You in faith, believing for a reward in seeking You. Jesus said that when we pray and believe, we will receive. _____ diligently seeks You and believes You will answer all prayers concerning (list concerns here). Some of these issues are as high a mountain, so as Jesus instructed, _____ tells that mountain to move out of the way. Lord, nothing is impossible for You. _____ asks all things in faith and without doubt. _____ will not grow weary in doing good or give up, but will reap a harvest in due season. Above all, _____ takes up the shield of faith to quench all the fiery darts of the wicked one, and thanks Christ Jesus who enables us and counts us faithful. _____ believes Your promises and sings Your praises. In Jesus' name I pray, Amen.

Fear, Worry, and Anxiety

Prepare Yourself

Be sure you have prayed through the Preparing to Petition the Courtroom of Heaven prayers in chapter ten. Include the Ambassador of Reconciliation prayer if you will be petitioning on behalf of others.

Prepare Your Case

Look up and meditate on these Scripture references: Psalm 118:28; Psalm 55:22; 2 Timothy 1:7; Philippians 4:6-7; 1 Peter 5:6-7; Matthew 6:34; John 14:27; 2 Thessalonians 3:16; Psalm 138:8

Add any additional Scriptures the Lord shows you.

Present a Petition for Yourself

I praise and exalt You, Lord, for Your name is worthy to be praised. I give all my burdens to You, and You take care of me. I will not be defeated. You did not give me a spirit of fear, but Your Spirit fills me with power, love, and a well-balanced mind. I do not worry about anything but pray about everything, thanking You for all You have done.

Lord, I humble myself under Your mighty hand, so that at the right time You will lift me up. Because You care for me, I give all my worries to You. (Take a moment to name all your concerns to the Lord.) I will not worry about tomorrow, for tomorrow will have its own worries and problems, as well as today.

Lord, You leave me with Your peace, which cannot be explained. It is not like the world gives. I will not let my heart be troubled or let it be afraid. The very Lord of peace Himself will comfort me in every way. Thank You for being with me today and every day. In Jesus' name I pray, Amen.

Present a Petition for Another

I praise and exalt You, Lord, for Your name is worthy to be praised. I pray that _____ will give every burden to You and that You will take care of him/her. _____ will not be defeated. You did not give _____ a spirit of fear, but a spirit of power, love, and a well-balanced mind. _____ will not worry about anything but will pray about everything, thanking You for all You have done.

Lord, at the right time you will lift up _____ as he/she humbles himself/herself under Your mighty hand. _____ gives every worry and care to You, because you care for _____. (Take a moment to list the concerns to the Lord.)

I pray that _____ will not worry about tomorrow, for tomorrow will have its own worries and problems, as well as today. Lord, may _____ experience Your unexplainable peace so his/her heart will not be troubled or afraid. The very Lord of peace Himself will give _____ peace in every way. Lord, thank You for being with _____ today and every day. In Jesus' name I pray, Amen.

Godly Acquaintances

Prepare Yourself

Be sure you have prayed through the Preparing to Petition the Courtroom of Heaven prayers in chapter ten. Include the Ambassador of Reconciliation prayer if you will be petitioning on behalf of others.

Prepare Your Case

Look up and meditate on these Scripture references: Psalm 118:28; Proverbs 12:26; Proverbs 14:6-7; Proverbs 13:20; Proverbs 4:14; Proverbs 24:21-22; Proverbs 22:24-25; 1 Corinthians 15:33; Luke 6:31; Romans 12:10; Proverbs 17:17; Proverbs 27:17

Add any additional Scriptures the Lord shows you.

Present a Petition for Yourself

You are my God, and I will praise You; You are my God and I will exalt you! Lord, Your Word tells me the righteous should choose friends carefully, for the way of the wicked leads us astray. I am to leave the presence of a foolish man when I perceive he lacks knowledge. May I be one who walks with wise men so I will be wise, for a companion of fools will be destroyed. Lord, keep me from entering the path of the wicked so I do not walk in the way of evil. Keep me from associating with those who rebel, for who knows what sudden calamity will come. Keep me from engaging in friendships with angry people so I do not become an angry person and set a snare for my soul. Bad company destroys good character. May I treat my friends as I desire them to treat me. May I be kind and affectionate to them with brotherly love, showing respect. May I be a friend who loves at all times. As iron sharpens iron, so a man sharpens the countenance of his friend. Thank You, Lord, for godly friends. May I always be a godly friend. In Jesus' name, Amen.

Present a Petition for Another

You are my God, and I will praise You; You are my God and I will exalt you. Lord, I pray that ____ will heed Your Word and choose friends carefully, for the way of the wicked leads us astray. I pray that ____ will leave the presence of foolish people who lack knowledge. I pray that ____ will be one who walks with wise men, for a companion of fools will be destroyed. Lord, keep ____ from entering the path of the wicked and walking in the way of evil. Keep ____ from associating with those who rebel, for who knows what sudden calamity will come. Keep ____ from engaging in friendships with angry people so that ____ does not become an angry person and set a snare for his/her soul. Bad company destroys good character. May ____ treat friends as he/she desires to be treated. May ____ be kind and affectionate to others with brotherly love, showing respect. May ____ be a friend who loves at all times. As iron sharpens iron, so a man sharpens the countenance of his friend. Thank You, Lord, for giving ____ godly friends. May ____ always be a godly friend to others. In Jesus' name, Amen.

Health and Healing

Prepare Yourself

Be sure you have prayed through the Preparing to Petition the Courtroom of Heaven prayers in chapter ten. Include the Ambassador of Reconciliation prayer if you will be petitioning on behalf of others.

Prepare Your Case

Look up and meditate on these Scripture references: Psalm 103:1-5; Exodus 15:26; Psalm 107:19-21; Psalm 41:2-3; James 5:16; 1 Peter 2:24

Add any additional Scriptures the Lord shows you.

Present a Petition for Yourself

Let all that I am praise the LORD; with my whole heart, I will praise his holy name. Let all that I am praise the LORD; may I never forget the good things he does for me. He forgives all my sins and heals all my diseases. He redeems me from death and crowns me with love and tender mercies. He fills my life with good things. My youth is renewed like the eagle's!

Lord, You promise that if I do what is right and follow Your commands, You will not allow me to suffer from any of the diseases You sent to the Egyptians, for You are the Lord my Healer. I cry out to You in my trouble, and You save me from my distress. You sent Your Word and healed me. You delivered me from my destruction. I give thanks to You, Lord, for Your lovingkindness. You promise to protect me and keep me alive, and I will be called blessed upon the earth. You will not give me over to the desires of my enemies. You sustain me on my sickbed and in my illness. You restore health to me, Lord. You tell me to confess my sins to another so that we can pray for each other. By doing this, I may be healed. The earnest prayer of a righteous man has a powerful effect. Thank You that Jesus Himself bore my sins in His body on the cross so that I might die to sin and live in righteousness, for by His wounds I am healed. Praise the Lord, my God and my Savior, who daily bears my burdens. In Jesus' name I pray, Amen.

Present a Petition for Another

Let all that I am praise the Lord; *with my whole heart, I will praise his holy name. Let all that I am praise the* Lord; *may I never forget the good things he does for me.*[4]

Lord, You forgive _____ of every sin and heal every disease. You redeem _____ from death and crown him/her with love and tender mercies. You fill _____'s life with good things so that his/her youth is renewed like the eagle's. You promise that if _____ does what is right and follows Your commands, You will not allow _____ to suffer from any of the diseases You sent to the Egyptians, for You are the Lord our Healer. I thank you that _____ cries out to You in trouble and You save _____ from all distress. You sent Your Word and healed _____. You delivered _____ from destruction. I give thanks to You, Lord, for Your lovingkindness.

You promise to keep alive and protect _____. I thank you that _____ will be called blessed upon the earth. Do not give _____ over to the desires of his/her enemies. You sustain _____ in his/her sickbed and in illness, restoring health. You tell _____ to confess every sin to another so they can pray for each other and be healed. The earnest prayer of a righteous man has a powerful effect. Lord, thank You that Jesus Himself bore _____'s sins in His body on the cross, so that _____ might die to sin and live in righteousness, for by His wounds _____ is healed. Praise the Lord, my God and my Savior, who daily bears _____'s burdens. In Jesus' name I pray, Amen.

Hope in the Lord

Prepare Yourself

Be sure you have prayed through the Preparing to Petition the Courtroom of Heaven prayers in chapter ten. Include the Ambassador of Reconciliation prayer if you will be petitioning on behalf of others.

Prepare Your Case

Look up and meditate on these Scripture references: Psalm 150:6; Ephesians 1:16-18; Psalm 37:4; Hebrews 11:1; 2 Corinthians 3:12; Psalm 71:14; Jeremiah 17:7-8; Psalm 31:24; Lamentations 3:25; Psalm 25:3

Add any additional Scriptures the Lord shows you.

Present a Petition for Yourself

I sing praises to the Lord! Father God, I ask You for spiritual wisdom and insight so that I will grow in my knowledge of You. I ask You to fill my heart with light so I can understand the confident hope You have given to me. Lord, I put my hope in You and keep Your ways. I place my faith in You, and my faith is the confidence that what I hope for will actually happen. I receive Your assurance about things I cannot see. Since I have such a glorious hope, with joyful and confident expectation, I speak freely, openly, and fearlessly. Blessed are those who trust in the Lord and made the Lord their hope and confidence. They are like a tree planted near the riverbank, roots running deep into the water. Such trees are not bothered by the heat or worried about the drought. Their leaves stay green and never stop producing fruit. I will be strong and take heart, hoping in You, Lord. For You are good to those whose hope is in You, to the one who seeks You. No one whose hope is in You will ever be put to shame. As for me, I will always have hope, and I will always praise You more and more. In Jesus' name I pray, Amen.

Present a Petition for Another

I sing praises to the Lord. Father God, I ask You to give _____ spiritual wisdom and insight to grow in the knowledge of You. Fill _____'s heart with light so he/she can understand the confident hope You have given to Your children. Lord, may _____ place all hope in You and keep Your ways. May _____ place his/her faith in You, believing with faith and confidence that what he/she hopes for will actually happen. May _____ receive Your assurance about things that cannot be seen. Since _____ has such a glorious hope, with joyful and confident expectation, _____can speak freely, openly, and fearlessly. Blessed are those who trust in the Lord and made the Lord their hope and confidence. They are like a tree planted near the riverbank, roots running deep into the water. Such trees are not bothered by the heat or worried about the drought. Their leaves stay green and never stop producing fruit. _____ shall be strong and take heart, hoping in You, Lord. For You are good to those whose hope is in You, to the one who seeks You. No one whose hope is in You will ever be put to shame. _____will always have hope and will always praise You more and more. In Jesus' name I pray, Amen.

Knowing God's Will

Prepare Yourself

Be sure you have prayed through the Preparing to Petition the Courtroom of Heaven prayers in chapter ten. Include the Ambassador of Reconciliation prayer if you will be petitioning on behalf of others.

Prepare Your Case

Look up and meditate on these Scripture references: Luke 11:2; John 6:40; Romans 12:1-2; 1 Thessalonians 5:16-18

Add any additional Scriptures the Lord shows you.

Present a Petition for Yourself

Lord, I bless Your holy name, the name above all names. I pray Your kingdom come and Your will to be done on earth as in heaven. I praise You that it is Your will for all who believe in Your Son, Jesus Christ, to have everlasting life. I pray that by the power of the Holy Spirit You draw close to You those whom I love who do not know Jesus as Lord. (Name those people here.) I pray that we will all be raised up together on the last day according to Your will. I present to You my body as a living sacrifice, holy and acceptable to You, which is my reasonable service. I do not want to be conformed to this world, but transformed by the renewing of my mind, so that I may prove what is Your good and acceptable and perfect will. I will always rejoice in You and pray without ceasing. I want all that I do to be like a prayer to You. Lord, I will give thanks in everything, because that is Your will for me. In Jesus' name I pray, Amen.

Present a Petition for Another

Lord, I bless Your holy name, the name above all names. I pray Your kingdom come and Your will be done on earth as it is in heaven. I praise You that it is Your will for _____ to believe in Your Son, Jesus Christ and have everlasting life. I pray that You draw _____ to You by the power of the Holy Spirit to know Jesus as Lord. I pray that we be raised up together on the last day according to Your will. I pray that _____ presents to You his/her body as a living sacrifice, holy and acceptable to You, which is our reasonable service. May _____ have no desire to be conformed to this world, but transformed by the renewing of the mind, in order to prove what is Your good and acceptable and perfect will. May _____ always rejoice in You and pray without ceasing. May everything _____ does be like a prayer to You. May _____ give thanks in everything, because that is Your will. In Jesus' name, Amen.

Knowing God's Purpose

Prepare Yourself

Be sure you have prayed through the Preparing to Petition the Courtroom of Heaven prayers in chapter ten. Include the Ambassador of Reconciliation prayer if you will be petitioning on behalf of others.

Prepare Your Case

Look up and meditate on these Scripture references: Psalm 51:5; Romans 12:1-2; Jeremiah 29:11; 2 Timothy 1:8-9; Ephesians 2:10; Ephesians 1:17-18; 1 Corinthians 15:58; Psalm 52:9
Add any additional Scriptures the Lord shows you.

Present a Petition for Yourself

O Lord, I open my lips and let my mouth declare praise to You, for the thoughts You think toward me are thoughts of peace and not of evil, to give me a future and a hope. For I am Your workmanship, created in Christ Jesus for good works, which You designed for me to walk in. I ask for the spirit of wisdom and revelation in the knowledge of You so that the eyes of my understanding will be enlightened. So I will know the hope of Your calling. I ask that You reveal to me Your perfect will, my specific calling that will glorify You. Then I will be steadfast, immovable, always abounding in the work of the Lord, knowing that my labor is not in vain. I will always praise You for all that You have done. In You I will hold on to hope, for Your name is good. In Jesus' name, Amen.

Present a Petition for Another

O Lord, I open my lips and let my mouth declare praise to You, for the thoughts You think toward _____ are thoughts of peace and not of evil, to give _____ a future and a hope. For _____ is Your workmanship, created in Christ Jesus for good works, which You designed for him/her to walk in. I ask You to give _____ the spirit of wisdom and revelation in the knowledge of You, that the eyes of _____'s understanding will be enlightened. May _____ know the hope of Your calling. Reveal Your perfect will and specific calling that will glorify You. Then _____ will be steadfast, immovable, always abounding in the work of the Lord, knowing that his/her labor is not in vain. I will always praise You for all that You have done. In You I will hold on to hope for Your name is good. In Jesus' name, Amen.

Peace

Prepare Yourself

Be sure you have prayed through the Preparing to Petition the Courtroom of Heaven prayers in chapter ten. Include the Ambassador of Reconciliation prayer if you will be petitioning on behalf of others.

Prepare Your Case

Look up and meditate on these Scripture references: Psalm 51:15; Psalm 85:8; Psalm 119:165; Isaiah 26:12; Isaiah 54:10; Isaiah 55:12; John 14:27; Romans 15:13

Add any additional Scriptures the Lord shows you.

Present a Petition for Yourself

Lord, I give all praise to You. You speak peace to me, one of Your faithful saints in Jesus. I love Your law and have great peace, so I do not stumble. You grant me peace as all my achievements are from You. The mountains may move and the hills disappear, but Your love for me will never end, nor Your promise of peace ever be removed from me. I will live in joy and peace. The mountains and the hills will burst into singing before me, and all the trees of the field will clap their hands in praise to the Creator. My heart will not be troubled, nor will it be afraid. May the God of hope fill me with all joy and peace in believing, so I may abound in hope by the power of the Holy Spirit. In Jesus' name, Amen.

Present a Petition for Another

Lord, I give all praise to You. I ask You to speak peace to _____, one of Your faithful saints in Jesus. _____ loves Your law, has great peace, and will not stumble. Grant _____ peace as all his/her achievements are from You. For the mountains may move and the hills disappear, but Your love for _____ will never end, nor Your promise of peace ever be removed. _____ will live in joy and peace. The mountains and the hills will burst into singing and all the trees of the field will clap their hands in praise to the Creator. _____'s heart will not be troubled, nor will it be afraid. May the God of hope fill _____ with all joy and peace, believing and abounding in hope by the power of the Holy Spirit. In Jesus' name, Amen.

Protection

Prepare Yourself

Be sure you have prayed through the Preparing to Petition the Courtroom of Heaven prayers in chapter ten. Include the Ambassador of Reconciliation prayer if you will be petitioning on behalf of others.

Prepare Your Case

Look up and meditate on this Scripture reference: Psalm 91
    Add any additional Scriptures the Lord shows you.

Present a Petition for Yourself

Father, I praise You and thank you that I will dwell in the secret place of the Most High and remain stable and fixed under the shadow of the Almighty, whose power no foe can withstand. I declare that You are my Refuge, my Fortress, my God. I will lean on and confidently trust in You, because You will deliver me from the snare of the fowler and from the deadly pestilence. You will cover me with Your feathers, where I will trust and find refuge under Your wings. Your truth and Your faithfulness are a shield and a buckler. I will not be afraid of the terror of the night, nor of the evil plots and slanders of the wicked. I will not fear the pestilence that stalks in darkness, nor the destruction and sudden death that surprise and lay waste at noonday. A thousand may fall at my side, and ten thousand at my right hand, but none of these curses will come near me. I will only be a spectator in the secret place of the Most High as I witness the reward of the wicked. Because I have made You my refuge and dwelling place, no evil will befall me, nor any plague or calamity come near my dwelling place. For You give Your angels charge over me, to accompany, defend, and preserve me in all my ways of obedience and service. Your angels will bear me up in their hands, so I won't dash my foot against a stone. I will tread upon and trample underfoot the young lion, the adder, and the serpent. Because I have set my love upon You, You will deliver me. You will set me on high, because I know and understand Your name. I have a personal knowledge of Your mercy, love, and kindness. I trust and rely on You, knowing You will never, ever forsake me. I will call upon You, and You will answer me. You are with me in trouble. You will deliver me and honor me, and with long life will You satisfy me and show me Your salvation. In Jesus' name, Amen.

Present a Petition for Another

Father, I praise You that _____ dwells in the secret place of the Most High and shall remain stable and fixed under the shadow of the Almighty, whose power no foe can withstand. You are _____'s Refuge, Fortress, and God. _____ will lean on and confidently trust in You. You will deliver _____ from the snare of the fowler and the deadly pestilence. You will cover _____ with Your feathers and give him/her refuge under Your wings. Your truth and Your faithfulness are a shield and a buckler. _____ will not be afraid of the terror of the night, nor of the evil plots and slanders of the wicked. _____ will not fear the pestilence that stalks in darkness, nor the destruction and sudden death that surprise and lay waste at noonday. A thousand may fall at _____'s side, and ten thousand at _____'s right hand, but none of these curses will come near him/her. _____ will only be a spectator in the secret place of the Most High as he/she witnesses the reward of the wicked. Because _____ has made You a refuge and dwelling place, there shall no evil befall _____ nor any plague or calamity come near. For You will give Your angels charge over _____ to accompany, defend, and preserve _____ in every act of obedience and service. Your angels will bear _____ up in their hands, so he/she will not dash a foot against a stone. _____ will tread upon and trample underfoot the young lion, adder, and serpent. Because _____ has set his/her love upon You, You will deliver and set on high _____, because _____ knows and understands Your name. _____ has a personal knowledge of Your mercy, love, and kindness. _____ trusts and relies on You, knowing You will never, ever forsake him/her. _____ will call upon You, and You will answer. You will be with _____ in trouble. You will deliver and honor _____, satisfying with long life and showing _____Your salvation. In Jesus' name, Amen.

Provision

Prepare Yourself

Be sure you have prayed through the Preparing to Petition the Courtroom of Heaven prayers in chapter ten. Include the Ambassador of Reconciliation prayer if you will be petitioning on behalf of others.

Prepare Your Case

Look up and meditate on these Scripture references: Isaiah 25:1; Genesis 22:14; Psalm 23:1-3; Psalm 34:10; Psalm 81:10; Psalm 84:11; Psalm 111:5; Matthew 6:33; Luke 12:24; Philippians 4:19; Psalm 66:2

Add any additional Scriptures the Lord shows you.

Present a Petition for Yourself

You are my God, O Lord! I praise Your name and give You honor. You have been faithful to carry out all Your plans. You are the Lord who provides. You are my Shepherd, and I have all I need. You give me rest in green meadows, and You lead me by peaceful streams. You renew my strength and guide me along the right paths, bringing honor to Your name. Even strong, young lions sometimes go hungry, but those who trust in You will never lack any good thing. For You, Lord, have rescued me from my Egypt. I open my mouth, and You fill it with good things. You do not refuse any good thing to those who do what is right. You give food to those who fear You, and You always remember Your covenant. Lord, I seek first Your kingdom above all else and live righteously. When I do, You provide me with everything I need. I see the ravens that do not plant or harvest or store food in barns, and You feed them. I am far more valuable to You than the birds. I thank You that You supply all my needs from Your glorious riches, which have been given to me in Christ Jesus. I sing glorious praises to You! In Jesus' name, Amen.

Present a Petition for Another

You are my God, O Lord! I praise Your name and give You honor. You have been faithful to carry out all Your plans. You are the Lord who provides. You are _____'s Shepherd, providing every need. You give _____ rest in green meadows, and You lead _____ by peaceful streams. You renew _____'s strength and guide _____along the right paths, bringing honor to Your name. Even strong, young lions sometimes go hungry, but _____ trusts in You and will never lack any good thing. For You have rescued _____from his/her Egypt. _____ opens his/her mouth, and You fill it with good things. You do not refuse any good thing to _____, who does what is right. You give food to _____, who fears You, and You always remember Your covenant. _____ seeks first Your kingdom above all else and lives righteously. You provide everything _____ needs. The ravens do not plant or harvest or store food in barns, and You feed them. _____ is far more valuable to You than the birds. Thank You that You supply all _____'s needs from Your glorious riches, which have been given to us in Christ Jesus. I sing glorious praises to You! In Jesus' name, Amen.

Restoration of Relationships

Prepare Yourself

Be sure you have prayed through the Preparing to Petition the Courtroom of Heaven prayers in chapter ten. Include the Ambassador of Reconciliation prayer if you will be petitioning on behalf of others.

Prepare Your Case

Look up and meditate on these Scripture references: Jeremiah 10:6-7; Colossians 3:13; Ephesians 4:31-32; Ecclesiastes 3:1; Philippians 2:3-4; John 14:27; Romans 12:18; Joel 2:25; Luke 10:27; 1 Corinthians 13:4-7

Add any additional Scriptures the Lord shows you.

Present a Petition for Yourself

> LORD, *there is no one like you! For you are great, and your name is full of power. Who would not fear you, O King of nations? That title belongs to you alone! Among all the wise people of the earth and in all the kingdoms of the world, there is no one like you.*[5]

Lord, I repent of my sins against _____ (list the things that caused hurt to someone you love such as yelling, accusations, withholding love, etc.).

Lord, Your Word says that if I have anything against anyone, I am to forgive him just as You forgive me. I desire to be obedient to Your Word. So, Father, in the

Name of Jesus Christ, as an act of my will, I choose to forgive _____ for _____.

I lay down all my hurt, my bitterness, and my anger in my relationship with _____. I ask for forgiveness for dishonoring _____with my words as I shared my hurt with others. From this point on, I desire to be kind and compassionate toward _____, forgiving just as You forgive me. Your Word says there is a right time for everything, and at the right time I desire to made amends with _____. I pray that in humility I will value _____ more than I value myself, placing the interest of others above my own.

I ask for the peace that only You can give. Because of Your peace, I will not let my heart be troubled, and I will not be afraid of the outcome of our relationship. I will live peaceably with _____. I ask You to restore all the years the swarming locusts have taken from this relationship. Lord, I declare today that I love You with all my heart, with all my soul, with all my strength, and with all my mind. And I love _____ as I love myself.

Love is patient and kind. Love is not jealous or boastful or proud or rude. It does not demand its own way. It is not irritable, and it keeps no record of being wronged. It does not rejoice about injustice but rejoices whenever the truth wins out. Love never gives up, never loses faith, is always hopeful, and endures through every circumstance.[6]

Present a Petition for Another

Lord, *there is no one like you! For you are great, and your name is full of power. Who would not fear you, O*

King of nations? That title belongs to you alone! Among all the wise people of the earth and in all the kingdoms of the world, there is no one like you.[7]

Lord, today I lift up _____ and ask that he/she will repent of any sins against _____. I pray _____ will honestly confess any sins and be forgiven by You.

Your Word says that if we have anything against anyone, we are to forgive them just as You forgive us. I pray that _____ will desire to be obedient to Your Word and will follow You. Father, in the Name of Jesus Christ, as an act of my will, I choose to forgive _____ for _____. I also pray that _____ will forgive those whom he/she is holding anything against.

I pray that _____ will lay down all hurts, all bitterness, and all anger in his/her relationship with _____. I pray that _____ will stop dishonoring _____ with words that have been shared with others. From this point on, I pray that _____ will desire to be kind and compassionate toward _____, forgiving just as You forgive.

Your Word says there is a right time for everything, and at the right time, I pray that _____ will desire to made amends with _____. I pray that in humility _____ will value _____ more than he/she values himself/herself, placing the interest of others above his/her own.

I ask for the peace that only You can give. Because of Your peace, I pray that _____'s heart will not be troubled, and _____ will not be afraid of the outcome of the relationship. I pray that _____ will live peaceably with _____. I ask You to restore all the years the swarming locusts have taken from _____ and _____. Lord, I declare today that _____ will love You with all his/her heart, soul, strength, and mind. I pray that _____ will love _____ as he/she loves himself/herself.

Love is patient and kind. Love is not jealous or boastful or proud or rude. It does not demand its own way. It is not irritable, and it keeps no record of being wronged. It does not rejoice about injustice but rejoices whenever the truth wins out. Love never gives up, never loses faith, is always hopeful, and endures through every circumstance.[8]

Turning Toward Christ

Prepare Yourself

Be sure you have prayed through the Preparing to Petition the Courtroom of Heaven prayers in chapter ten. Include the Ambassador of Reconciliation prayer if you will be petitioning on behalf of others.

Prepare Your Case

Look up and meditate on these Scripture references: John 3:16; Luke 19:10; 2 Thessalonians 2:13; 2 Corinthians 6:2; Acts 4:12; Psalm 27:1: Psalm 118:21

Add any additional Scriptures the Lord shows you.

Present a Petition for Yourself

Lord, You said whoever believes in You will not die but have eternal life. Because I believe in You, I will not perish but have eternal life with You. You came to seek and save the lost. I am thankful, for I am loved by You. You chose me from the beginning for salvation that comes through the Spirit, who makes me holy through my belief in the truth. At just the right time, You have heard me, and in the day of salvation, You have helped me. Today is the day I receive Your deliverance, preservation, and find safety in You. Salvation comes only through Jesus Christ, for there is no other name under heaven by which I can be saved. The Lord is my light and my salvation, and I will never be afraid. You are my victorious redeemer. I thank You and praise You. In Jesus' name, Amen.

Present a Petition for Another

Lord, You said whoever believes in You will not die but have eternal life. I pray that _____ believes in You and will not perish but have eternal life with You. You have come to seek and save the lost. I am thankful that _____ is loved by You. You chose _____ from the beginning for salvation that comes through the Spirit, who makes us holy through belief in the truth. At just the right time, You have heard us, and in the day of salvation, You have helped us. Today is the day _____ receives Your deliverance, preservation, and finds safety in You. Salvation comes only through Jesus Christ, for there is no other name under heaven by which _____ can be saved. The Lord is _____'s light and salvation, and _____ will never have to be afraid. You are _____'s victorious redeemer. I thank You and praise You. In Jesus' name, Amen.

Guided by Truth

Prepare Yourself

Be sure you have prayed through the Preparing to Petition the Courtroom of Heaven prayers in chapter ten. Include the Ambassador of Reconciliation prayer if you will be petitioning on behalf of others.

Prepare Your Case

Look up and meditate on these Scripture references: Psalm 43:3-4; 2 Timothy 3:16-17; John 17:17; John 8:32; John 16:13; Colossians 2:8

Add any additional Scriptures the Lord shows you.

Present a Petition for Yourself

Send out your light and your truth; let them guide me. Let them lead me to your holy mountain, to the place where you live. There I will go to the altar of God, to God—the source of all my joy. I will praise you with my harp, O God, my God![P]

Lord, the whole Bible was inspired by You. It teaches me what is true and to understand what is wrong in my life. The Bible gives me instruction and correction, showing me the path to do what is right. You use Your Word to prepare me to do good works. I ask You to make me holy by Your Word, which is truth. Jesus is the way, the truth, and the life, and the only way I can come to You is through Him. I choose to embrace

Your truth that sets me free. The Spirit of truth guides me into all truth, and He only says what He hears from the Father. He will tell me about my future. Do not let anyone distract me and lead me astray with human logic and spiritual powers of this world that are not of Christ. Thank You, Lord. In Jesus' name, Amen.

Present a Petition for Another

Send out your light and your truth; let them guide me. Let them lead me to your holy mountain, to the place where you live. There I will go to the altar of God, to God—the source of all my joy. I will praise you with my harp, O God, my God![10]

Lord, the whole Bible was inspired by You. It teaches _____ what is true and to understand what is wrong in his/her life. The Bible gives _____ instruction and correction, showing the path to do what is right. You use Your Word to prepare _____ to do good works. I ask You to make _____ holy by Your Word, which is truth. Jesus is the way, the truth, and the life and the only way _____ can come to You is through Him. _____ chooses to embrace Your truth, and the truth sets him/her free. The Spirit of truth guides _____ into all truth, and He only says what He hears from the Father. He will tell _____ about the future. Do not let anyone distract _____ and lead him/her astray with human logic and spiritual powers of this world that are not of Christ. Thank You Lord. Thank you, Lord. In Jesus' name, Amen.

Serve the Lord

Prepare Yourself

Be sure you have prayed through the Preparing to Petition the Courtroom of Heaven prayers in chapter ten. Include the Ambassador of Reconciliation prayer if you will be petitioning on behalf of others.

Prepare Your Case

Look up and meditate on these Scripture references: 1 Samuel 12:24; Joshua 22:5; 1 Chronicles 28:9; 2 Chronicles 15:7; Galatians 5:13; Hebrews 9:14; John 12:26; Romans 12:11; Mark 10:45; 1 Peter 4:10

Add any additional Scriptures the Lord shows you.

Present a Petition for Yourself

Sing praises to God and to his name! Sing loud praises to him who rides the clouds. His name is the LORD—*rejoice in his presence!*[1]

Lord, I trust in You. I faithfully serve You as I think about all the wonderful things You have done for me. I want to be careful to obey all Your commands, to love You, to walk in all of Your ways, to cling to You, and to serve You enthusiastically. You see my heart and know my very plan and thought. You promise that if I seek You, I will find You. I will continue to keep up the good work and not let myself get discouraged, for You will reward me. Through Jesus I am able to live in freedom, but I will not use freedom as an excuse to make wrong choices. I will use my freedom to serve others, in love. I have been cleansed by the blood of the Lamb from dead works so I may serve the living God. May I be a servant of Christ, not lagging in diligence, fervent in spirit, serving the Lord. For even Jesus, the Son of Man, did not come to be served, but to serve. He gave His life as a ransom for many. Since I have received this gift from God, I will use it well to serve others. Thank You, Lord. In Jesus' name, Amen.

Present a Petition for Another

Sing praises to God and to his name! Sing loud praises to him who rides the clouds. His name is the LORD—rejoice in his presence![12]

Lord, I trust in You. I faithfully serve You as I think about all the wonderful things You have done. I pray that _____ wants to be careful to obey all Your commands, to love You, to walk in all of Your ways, to cling to You, and to serve You enthusiastically. You see _____'s heart and know every plan and thought. You promise that if _____ seeks You, you will be found. I pray _____ will continue to keep up the good work and not get discouraged, for You will reward him/her. Through Jesus, _____ is able to live in freedom, but that freedom will not be used as an excuse to make wrong choices. _____ will use his/her freedom to serve others, in love. _____ has been cleansed by the blood of the Lamb from dead works in order to serve the living God. May _____ be a servant of Christ, not lagging in diligence, fervent in spirit, serving the Lord. For even Jesus, the Son of Man, did not come to be served, but to serve. He gave His life as a ransom for many. Since _____ has received this gift from God, it will be used well to serve others. Thank You, Lord. In Jesus' name, Amen.

Slow to Anger

Prepare Yourself

Be sure you have prayed through the Preparing to Petition the Courtroom of Heaven prayers in chapter ten. Include the Ambassador of Reconciliation prayer if you will be petitioning on behalf of others.

Prepare Your Case

Look up and meditate on these Scripture references: Psalm 5:11; Ephesians 4:26-27, 29-31; James 1:19-20; Proverbs 29:11; Proverbs 14:29; Proverbs 19:11; Proverbs 15:1; Colossians 3:8; Psalm 37:8-9; Colossians 3:15

Add any additional Scriptures the Lord shows you.

Present a Petition for Yourself

> *But let all who take refuge in you rejoice; let them sing joyful praises forever. Spread your protection over them, that all who love your name may be filled with joy.*[13]

Lord, Your Word instructs me not to nurse a grudge or let my anger control me. Neither am I to let the sun go down while I am still angry, or it will allow the accuser an opportunity to hinder my petitions in the courtroom of heaven. May I refrain from bad language and only say what is good and helpful so that I encourage others. I do not want to cause the Holy Spirit sorrow by the way I live, for He has identified me as His own, guaranteeing that I will be saved on the day of redemption. I will listen more to others and refrain from speaking too much. I will not become angry, for anger does not promote God's righteous purpose in me. I will be wise by holding back my urge to vent so I will have great understanding. As a wise person demonstrating patience and controlling my temper, I will earn respect for overlooking the wrongs against me. When I respond gently, I will defuse the rage of another. For anger will ruin my testimony in the courtroom of heaven. I rid myself of all anger, rage, hatred, cursing, and filthy language. I will trust in You so I may receive Your blessings. I allow the peace that comes from Christ to guide my heart, for I am a part of His body. I will always be thankful. In Jesus' name, Amen.

Present a Petition for Another

But let all who take refuge in you rejoice; let them sing joyful praises forever. Spread your protection over them, that all who love your name may be filled with joy.[14]

Lord, Your Word instructs _____ not to nurse a grudge or allow anger to control him/her. Neither is _____ to let the sun go down while still angry, or it will allow the accuser an opportunity to hinder any petitions in the courtroom of heaven. May _____ refrain from bad language and only say what is good and helpful to encourage others. _____ does not want to cause the Holy Spirit sorrow by the way he/she lives, for He has identified _____ as His own, guaranteeing salvation on the day of redemption. _____ will listen more to others and refrain from speaking too much. _____ will not become angry, for anger does not promote God's righteous purpose. _____ will be wise and have great understanding by holding back the urge to vent. As a wise person who demonstrates patience and controls his/her temper, _____ will earn respect for overlooking the wrongs against him/her. When _____ responds gently, it will defuse the rage of another. For anger will ruin any testimony in the courtroom of heaven. So, _____ will get rid of all anger, rage, hatred, cursing, and filthy language. _____ will trust in You in order to receive Your blessings. _____ is a part of Your body and allows the peace that comes from Christ to guide his/her heart. _____ will always be thankful. In Jesus' name, Amen.

Strength

Prepare Yourself

Be sure you have prayed through the Preparing to Petition the Courtroom of Heaven prayers in chapter ten. Include the Ambassador of Reconciliation prayer if you will be petitioning on behalf of others.

Prepare Your Case

Look up and meditate on these Scripture references: Psalm 9:1-2; Isaiah 40:29-31; Habakkuk 3:19; Psalm 118:14; Psalm 119:28; Psalm 46:1; Nehemiah 8:10; Psalm 22:19; Psalm 28:7-8; 2 Corinthians 12:9-10; Philippians 4:13; Ephesians 6:10

Add any additional Scriptures the Lord shows you.

Present a Petition for Yourself

> *I will praise you, LORD, with all my heart; I will tell of all the marvelous things you have done. I will be filled with joy because of you. I will sing praises to your name, O Most High.*[15]

Lord, You give power to the weak and strengthen those who lack power. Even the youth get tired and worn out, and the young men stumble and fall. But those who trust in You will find new strength. They will mount up on wings like eagles. They will run and not be weary. They will walk and not faint. You make me as surefooted as a deer, able to climb mountains. You are my strength and song, and You give me victory.

When my soul melts from heaviness, strengthen me according to Your Word. You are my refuge and strength, always ready to help me in time of trouble. Joy rises up in my heart and bursts out in praise to You, for the joy of the Lord is my strength. You are my shield. My heart trusts in You, and I am helped. God, Your grace is sufficient for me, and Your strength is made perfect in my weakness. I will celebrate my weaknesses for then the power of Christ will be demonstrated in my life. When I am surrounded by troubles and face persecutions all around me, I am made stronger. My weakness becomes an entrance for Your power. I can do all things through Christ who gives me strength. In Christ I am infused with strength and stand victorious with His power flowing in and through me. Thank You, Lord, for renewed strength today. In Jesus' name, Amen.

Present a Petition for Another

I will praise you, Lord, with all my heart; I will tell of all the marvelous things you have done. I will be filled with joy because of you. I will sing praises to your name, O Most High.[16]

Lord, You give power to the weak and strengthen those who lack power. Even the youth get tired and worn out, and the young men stumble and fall. But those who trust in the Lord will find new strength. They will mount up on wings like eagles. They will run and not be weary. They will walk and not faint. You make _____ as surefooted as a deer, able to climb mountains. You are _____'s strength and song. You give _____ victory. When _____'s soul melts from heaviness, you give strength according to Your Word. You are _____'s refuge, always ready to help in times of trouble. Joy rises up in _____'s heart and bursts out in praise to You, for the joy of the Lord is our source of strength. You, Lord, are _____'s shield. _____'s heart trusts in You and is helped. God, Your grace is sufficient for _____, and Your strength is made perfect in weakness. _____will celebrate his/her weaknesses for then the power of Christ will be demonstrated. When _____ is surrounded by troubles and faces persecutions all around, he/she is made stronger. _____'s weakness becomes an entrance for Your power. _____ can do all things through Christ who gives us strength. In Christ, _____ is infused with strength and stands victorious with Your power flowing in and through him/her. Thank You, Lord, for renewing _____'s strength today. In Jesus' name, Amen.

Trusting God

Prepare Yourself

Be sure you have prayed through the Preparing to Petition the Courtroom of Heaven prayers in chapter ten. Include the Ambassador of Reconciliation prayer if you will be petitioning on behalf of others.

Prepare Your Case

Look up and meditate on these Scripture references: 2 Samuel 7:28; Psalm 9:10; Psalm 13:5; Psalm 56:3; Psalm 84:12; Proverbs 3:5-6; John 14:1

Add any additional Scriptures the Lord shows you.

Present a Petition for Yourself

You are my God, and I will praise You! You are my God and I will exalt you![17]

Thank You, Lord, for You have let me experience Your mercy. I will keep putting my trust in You. I can count on You for help, because You will never neglect me when I come to You. I trust in Your kindness and will celebrate with passion and joy because You rescue me. When I am afraid, I will trust in You with all of my heart, for blessed are those who trust in You. I trust completely in You, my Lord, and do not rely on my own reasoning and logic. I seek Your will in all I do, so You can lead me in every decision I make. I will not give in to my fears, for I trust God and believe in

Jesus. Thank You, Lord, for giving me confident trust in You. In Jesus' name, Amen.

Present a Petition for Another

You are my God, and I will praise You! You are my God and I will exalt you![18]

Thank You, Lord, for You have let _____ experience Your mercy. As a result, _____ will keep putting his/her trust in You. _____ can count on You for help, for You will never neglect your children when they come to You. _____ trusts in Your kindness and will celebrate with passion and joy because You rescue him/her. When _____ is afraid, he/she will trust in You wholeheartedly, for blessed are those who trust in You. _____ does not rely on human reasoning and logic. _____ seeks Your will in all things so You will lead in every decision he/she makes. _____ will not give in to fear for _____ trusts You and believes in Jesus. Thank You, Lord, for giving _____ confident trust in You. In Jesus' name, Amen.

Using Gifts from God

Prepare Yourself

Be sure you have prayed through the Preparing to Petition the Courtroom of Heaven prayers in chapter ten. Include the Ambassador of Reconciliation prayer if you will be petitioning on behalf of others.

Prepare Your Case

Look up and meditate on these Scripture references: Psalm 145:3; James 1:17; Romans 11:29; Ephesians 4:7-8; Ephesians 4:11-13; 2 Timothy 1:6; 1 Peter 4:10-11; Colossians 3:23-24; Romans 12:11

Add any additional Scriptures the Lord shows you.

Present a Petition for Yourself

Lord, You are great and worthy of my highest praise. Your greatness is beyond my understanding. I thank You for freely giving me good and perfect gifts. And whatever You choose to give me can never be taken away. Through Your generosity, You gave everything You promised after Christ returned triumphantly to heaven and defeated Satan. You gave to the church apostles, prophets, evangelists, pastors, and teachers so that I will be nurtured and prepared to do my part to build up the body of Christ. I will continue to stir up the gifts You have imparted to me. I will use them to serve others with all the strength and energy You give me. I will work willingly and cheerfully in all You lead me to do as I am doing it for You, not just to please other people. I ask You to bless me with spiritual gifts so that I may use them to bless others and expand the kingdom of God. In Jesus' name, Amen.

Present a Petition for Another

Lord, You are great and worthy of my highest praise. Your greatness is beyond understanding. I thank You for freely giving _____ good and perfect gifts that can never be taken away. Through Your generosity, You gave everything You promised after Christ returned triumphantly to heaven and defeated Satan. You gave to the church apostles, prophets, evangelists, pastors, and teachers so that _____ will be nurtured and prepared to build up the body of Christ. _____ will continue to stir up the gifts You have imparted and will use those gifts to serve others with all the strength and energy You give. _____ will work willingly and cheerfully in all You lead him/her to do, because it is being done for You, not just to please other people. I ask You to bless _____ with spiritual gifts in order to use them to bless others and expand the kingdom of God. In Jesus' name, Amen.

Walking in the Spirit

Prepare Yourself

Be sure you have prayed through the Preparing to Petition the Courtroom of Heaven prayers in chapter ten. Include the Ambassador of Reconciliation prayer if you will be petitioning on behalf of others.

Prepare Your Case

Look up and meditate on these Scripture references: John 4:21-24; Romans 8:1-17; Galatians 5:16-25

Add any additional Scriptures the Lord shows you.

Present a Petition for Yourself

The time has come when all worshippers will worship the Father in Spirit and truth. Since You, God, are a Spirit, I will worship You in Spirit and truth. I am in Christ Jesus, and I cannot be condemned. The accusing voice of condemnation has been silenced, for the Spirit has empowered me to be free from the vicious cycle of sin and death. I live a life filled by the Holy Spirit, so I do what pleases God. The Spirit leads me to life and peace. The Spirit of Resurrection lives in me and gives life to my mortal body. When I received the Spirit, I was adopted as Your very own child, and I am now part of the family of God. I will never feel like an orphan as my spirit is joined with Yours. You are my beloved Father. I walk and live in the Spirit, so I bear the fruit of the Spirit, which is love, joy, peace, longsuffering, kindness, goodness, faithfulness, gentleness, and self-control. I will continue to live in the Spirit and follow after You. In Jesus' name, Amen.

Present a Petition for Another

The time has come when all worshippers will worship the Father in Spirit and truth. Since God is Spirit, _____ will worship You in Spirit and truth. _____ is in Christ Jesus and cannot be condemned. The accusing voice of condemnation has been silenced, for the Spirit has empowered _____ to be free from the vicious cycle of sin and death. _____ lives a life filled by the Holy Spirit and does what pleases You. The Spirit leads _____ to life and peace. The Spirit of Resurrection lives inside _____ and gives life to his/her mortal body. Because _____ received the Spirit and was adopted as God's very own child, _____ is now part of the family of God. _____ will never feel like an orphan, because his/her spirit is joined with Yours. You are _____'s beloved Father. _____ walks and lives in the Spirit, and bears the Fruit of the Spirit, which is love, joy, peace, kindness, longsuffering, goodness, faithfulness, gentleness, and self-control. _____ will continue to live in the Spirit and follow after You. In Jesus' name, Amen.

Walking Humbly with God

Prepare Yourself

Be sure you have prayed through the Preparing to Petition the Courtroom of Heaven prayers in chapter ten. Include the Ambassador of Reconciliation prayer if you will be petitioning on behalf of others.

Prepare Your Case

Look up and meditate on these Scripture references: 1 Peter 1:3; Proverbs 15:33; Psalm 25:8-9; Micah 6:8; Proverbs 22:4; Ephesians 4:2; Philippians 2:3; James 4:10; 1 Peter 5:6; 1 Peter 3:8; Philippians 4:20

Add any additional Scriptures the Lord shows you.

Present a Petition for Yourself

I give praise to You, Lord, for Your great mercy and for giving me the privilege of a new life so I can live with great expectation through the resurrected life of Christ. My humility and reverence for You is my source of revelation knowledge. You are good, for You show me the right path, even when I go astray. When I remain humble, You lead on the right path and teach me Your ways. Your Word tells me what You want from me: to do what is right, to love mercy, and to walk humbly in Your ways. True humility will lead me to riches, honor, and a long life. I will always be humble and gentle, showing love toward those who try my patience. I refuse to be selfish. In humility, I will put others first and view them as more important than myself. I humble myself before You, and You will lift me up in due time. I desire to live in harmony with others, to be tenderhearted, and to keep a humble attitude in this life. In Jesus' name, Amen.

Present a Petition for Another

I give praise to You, Lord, for Your great mercy and for giving us the privilege of a new life so we can live with great expectation through the resurrected life of Christ. _____'s humility and reverence for You is the source of revelation knowledge. You are good, for You show _____ the right path, even when _____ goes astray. When _____ remains humble, You lead him/her on the right path and teach him/her Your ways. Your Word tells _____ what You want: to do what is right, to love mercy, and to walk humbly in Your ways. True humility will lead _____ to riches, honor, and a long life. _____ will always be humble and gentle, showing love toward those who try his/her patience. _____ refuses to be selfish. In humility, _____ will put others first and view them as more important. As _____ humbles himself/herself before You, You will lift _____ up in due time. _____ desires to live in harmony with others, to be tenderhearted, and to keep a humble attitude in this life. In Jesus' name, Amen.

Where to Live

Prepare Yourself

Be sure you have prayed through the Preparing to Petition the Courtroom of Heaven prayers in chapter ten. Include the Ambassador of Reconciliation prayer if you will be petitioning on behalf of others.

Prepare Your Case

Look up and meditate on these Scripture references: Psalm 106:1; Acts 17:26; Deuteronomy 32:8; Psalm 105:1-2

Add any additional Scriptures the Lord shows you.

Present a Petition for Yourself

I praise You, Lord. I give thanks to You, for You are God, and Your mercy never ends. Your Word says that from one man You made all nations of men to inhabit the whole earth. You determined the time I was to be born and have selected the place where I will live. If where I am living was my choice and not Yours, I ask that You move me to the place where I should live. When You gave Israel their inheritance, You separated them by tribes and set their boundaries. As I receive my inheritance in Christ, I seek to live within the boundaries You established for me. I sing praises to You, and I will share about all Your wonderful works in my life. In Jesus' name, Amen.

Present a Petition for Another

I praise You, Lord. I give thanks to You, for You are God, and Your mercy never ends. Your Word says that from one man You made all nations of men to inhabit the whole earth. You determined the time _____ was to be born and have selected the place where _____ will live. If where _____ is living was not Your choice, I ask that You move _____ to the place you have chosen. When You gave Israel their inheritance, You separated them by tribes and set their boundaries. As _____ receives his/her inheritance in Christ, _____ seeks to live within the boundaries You have established. _____ will sing praises to You and share about all Your wonderful works. In Jesus' name, Amen.

Who I Am in Christ

Prepare Yourself

Be sure you have prayed through the Preparing to Petition the Courtroom of Heaven prayers in chapter ten. Include the Ambassador of Reconciliation prayer if you will be petitioning on behalf of others.

Prepare Your Case

Look up and meditate on these Scripture references: Psalm 86:10; Romans 8:16; Ephesians 1:4; 1 Peter 1:23; 2 Corinthians 5:17; 2 Corinthians 3:18; Philippians 1:6; 1 Corinthians 6:19; 1 Corinthians 2:16; Colossians 1:13; Romans 6:11; 1 John 5:18; Colossians 2:7; Matthew 16:20; 1 John 4:4; John 14:12-14; 1 John 4:17; Ephesians 1:19-20

Add any additional Scriptures the Lord shows you.

Present a Petition for Yourself

You alone are God. You are great and do amazing things. I am Your child. You chose me before the world was created to live a holy life in Christ. I am born again into a life that will last forever for it comes from the eternal, living Word of God. I am a new creation in Christ Jesus, and my new life has begun. By the Spirit, I am being transformed into Your image. You began this good work in me and will bring it to completion. I am the temple of the Holy Spirit. I have the mind of Christ. I have been delivered from the control and dominion of the Devil and have been transferred into the kingdom of love. I am dead to sin and made alive in Christ. Because I am born of God, the evil one cannot touch me. I am firmly rooted, built up, and established in my faith. I have faith that can move mountains. Greater is He who lives in me than he who is in the world. Because I believe, trust, and rely on You, I can do the things Jesus did, and even greater things will I do, for His Spirit within me knows no limit. As Jesus is, so am I in this world. The immeasurable, unlimited, and surpassing power of God—the same resurrection power that raised Jesus from the dead—lives on the inside of me. In Jesus' name, Amen.

Present a Petition for Another

You alone are God. You are great and do amazing things. _____ is God's child. You chose_____ before the world was created to live a holy life in Christ. _____ is born again into a life that will last forever for it comes from the eternal, living Word of God. _____ is a new creation in Christ Jesus and a new life has begun. By the Spirit, _____ is being transformed into Your image. You began this good work in _____ and will finish it. _____ is the temple of the Holy Spirit and has the mind of Christ. _____ has been delivered from the control and dominion of the Devil and has been transferred into the kingdom of love. _____ is dead to sin and made alive in Christ. _____ is born of God and cannot be touched by the evil one. _____ is firmly rooted, built up, and established and has faith that can move mountains. Greater is He who lives in _____ than he who is in the world. Because _____ believes, trusts, and relies on You, _____ can do the things Jesus did and even greater, for the Spirit within has no limit. As Jesus is, so is _____ in this world. The immeasurable, unlimited, and surpassing power of God—the same resurrection power that raised Jesus from the dead—lives on the inside of _____. In Jesus' name, Amen.

Wisdom and Knowledge

Prepare Yourself

Be sure you have prayed through the Preparing to Petition the Courtroom of Heaven prayers in chapter ten. Include the Ambassador of Reconciliation prayer if you will be petitioning on behalf of others.

Preparing Your Case

Look up and meditate on these Scripture references: Psalm 147:1; James 1:5; James 3:17; Ephesians 5:15-17; Proverbs 3:13; Ephesians 1:17; Proverbs 1:7; Proverbs 4:7; Proverbs 16:16

Add any additional Scriptures the Lord shows you.

Present a Petition for Yourself

How delightful and fitting it is to sing praises to You. Lord, Your Word says if I want to be wise, I can ask You for wisdom, and You will give it to me. I'm asking for wisdom today, for Your wisdom is first of all pure. It is also peaceable, gentle, willing to yield, full of mercy and good fruits, has no partiality, and shows no favoritism. I desire to be careful how I live, not as a fool, but as the wise. The person who finds wisdom has joy and gains understanding. Father of glory, I ask You to give me the Spirit of wisdom and insight so I may grow in my knowledge of Christ, for the fear of the Lord is the beginning of knowledge. Since getting wisdom is the best thing I can do, I desire it now, for it is much better than acquiring gold or silver. I thank You today for giving me godly wisdom. In Jesus' name, Amen.

Present a Petition for Another

How delightful and fitting it is to sing praises to You. Lord, Your Word says if _____ wants to be wise, he/she can ask You for wisdom and You will give it. On behalf of _____, I'm asking You to impart wisdom today, for Your wisdom is first of all pure. It is also peaceable, gentle, willing to yield, full of mercy and good fruits, has no partiality, and shows no favoritism. I believe _____ desires to be careful in how he/she lives, not as a fool, but as the wise. The person who finds wisdom has joy and gains understanding. Father of glory, I ask You to give _____ the Spirit of wisdom and insight in order to grow in the knowledge of Christ. For the fear of the Lord is the beginning of knowledge. Since getting wisdom is the wisest thing _____ can do, I pray that _____ receives it now, for it is much better than acquiring gold or silver. I thank You today for giving _____ wisdom. In Jesus' name, Amen.

Youth Renewed

Prepare Yourself

Be sure you have prayed through the Preparing to Petition the Courtroom of Heaven prayers in chapter ten. Include the Ambassador of Reconciliation prayer if you will be petitioning on behalf of others.

Prepare Your Case

Look up and meditate on these Scripture references: Psalm 103:1-5; Proverbs 4:23; Ephesians 4:23; Romans 8:2; Psalm 92:14; Isaiah 40:29-31

Add any additional Scriptures the Lord shows you.

Present a Petition for Yourself

Let all that I am praise the LORD; WITH MY WHOLE HEART, I WILL PRAISE HIS HOLY NAME. *Let all that I am praise the* LORD; *may I never forget the good things he does for me. He forgives all my sins and heals all my diseases. He redeems me from death and crowns me with love and tender mercies. He fills my life with good things. My youth is renewed like the eagle's!*[19]

Father, I guard my heart above all else, for it determines the course of my life. I allow the Spirit to renew my thoughts and my attitudes. Because I belong to You, the power of the life-giving Spirit has freed me from the power of sin that leads to death. As I age, I will stay fresh and continue to produce fruit. You give power to the weak and strength to the powerless. Even the youth become weak and tired, and young men become exhausted. I will trust in You, Lord, and find new strength. I will soar high on wings like eagles. I will run and not grow weary. I will walk and not faint. This I pray in Jesus' name, Amen.

Present a Petition for Another

May _____ praise Your name wholeheartedly. May _____ never forget the good things You do for him/her. You forgive all _____'s sins and heal all _____'s diseases. You redeem _____ from death and crown him/her with love and tender mercies. You fill _____'s life with good things, and _____'s youth is renewed like the eagle. _____ guards his/her heart above all else, for it determines the course of life. _____ allows the Spirit to renew all thoughts and attitudes. Because _____ belongs to You, Lord, the power of the life-giving Spirit has freed _____ from the power of sin that leads to death. As _____ ages, he/she will stay fresh and continue to produce fruit. The Lord gives power to the weak and strength to the powerless. Even youth become weak and tired, and young men become exhausted. _____ will trust in You and will find new strength. _____ will soar high on wings like eagles and will run and not grow weary. _____ will walk and not faint. This I pray in Jesus' name, Amen.

Favor with the Prison Warden

Prepare Yourself

Be sure you have prayed through the Preparing to Petition the Courtroom of Heaven prayers in chapter ten.

Preparing Your Case

Look up and meditate on these Scripture references: 1 Chronicles 16:8; Genesis 39:21; Proverbs 3:3-4; Proverbs 8:32-35; Proverbs 12:2; Luke 2:52; Psalm 145:3

Add any additional Scriptures the Lord shows you.

Inmate Petition

> I give thanks to You, Lord, and call upon Your name, making known all Your glorious deeds among the people. Just as You were with Joseph and gave him favor with the prison warden, I ask You to be with me and extend kindness to me, granting me favor with the prison warden and correction officers. I tie loyalty and faithfulness around my neck and write them on my heart so that I will find favor with both God and with people, earning a good reputation. I listen to You, and I'm blessed for keeping Your ways. I receive Your instruction so I will be wise and careful not to ignore it. When I find wisdom, I obtain favor from You. I continually increase in wisdom and stature and in favor with God and man. Great is the Lord and highly to be praised. In Jesus' name, Amen.

Family of Inmate Petition

I give thanks to You, Lord, and call upon Your name, making known all Your glorious deeds among the people. Just as You were with Joseph and gave him favor with the prison warden, I ask You to be with _____ and extend kindness by granting _____ favor with the prison warden and correction officers. _____ ties loyalty and faithfulness around his/her neck and writes them on his/her heart in order to find favor with both God and with people, earning a good reputation.

_____ listens to You and is blessed for keeping Your ways. _____ receives Your instruction and will be wise and careful not to ignore it. _____ finds wisdom and obtains favor from You. _____ continually increases in wisdom and stature and in favor with God and man. Great is the Lord and highly to be praised. In Jesus' name, Amen.

For Those in Authority

Prepare Yourself

Be sure you have prayed through the Preparing to Petition the Courtroom of Heaven prayers in chapter ten.

Preparing Your Case

Look up and meditate on these Scripture references: 2 Timothy 3:16; 1 Timothy 2:1-2; Psalm 86:3; Ephesians 1:17; James 1:5; Matthew 6:13; Philippians 4:19; Proverbs 11:3

Add any additional Scriptures the Lord shows you.

Inmate Petition

Lord, I thank You, for Your Word teaches me how to live. I come before You today as instructed by You to lift up supplications, prayers, and intercessions. I give thanks for the warden and correction officers who are in authority over (name of prison) where I live. I ask You to have mercy on them, and I thank You for all that You will do for them. Lord, I ask that You guide them in Your knowledge and understanding, giving them wisdom for each situation they face. I ask You to protect them from the evil one and meet all their needs according to Your glorious riches in Christ Jesus. I pray they serve You with integrity and honesty. As I pray for those who are in authority over me, I ask that they be able to live in peace and quietness so I can spend my time inside living a godly life and serving You wholeheartedly. In Jesus' name, Amen.

Family of Inmate Petition

Lord, I thank You, for Your Word teaches me how
to live. I come before You today as instructed by You
to lift up supplications, prayers, and intercessions.
I give thanks for the warden and correction officers
who are in authority over (name of prison) where
(name of person praying for) lives. I ask You to have
mercy on those in authority there, and I thank You for
all You will do for them. Lord, I ask that You guide
them in Your knowledge and understanding, giving
them wisdom for each situation they face. I ask You
to protect them from the evil one and meet all their
needs according to Your glorious riches in Christ Jesus.
I pray they serve You with integrity and honesty. As I
pray for those in authority at (name of prison) and
those who preside over _____, I ask that _____ will
be able to live in peace and quietness so he/she can
spend the time inside living a godly life and serving
You wholeheartedly. In Jesus' name, Amen.

Welfare of the Prison

Prepare Yourself

Be sure you have prayed through the Preparing to Petition the Courtroom of Heaven prayers in chapter ten.

Preparing Your Case

Look up and meditate on these Scripture references: 2 Timothy 3:16; Jeremiah 29:7; Numbers 6:24-26; Colossians 3:15; Ephesians 4:3; Isaiah 26:3; Jeremiah 29:7

Add any additional Scriptures the Lord shows you.

Inmate Petition

> Lord, I thank You that Your Word directs me and teaches me what to do. Today, I lift up in prayer (name of prison) where I am exiled. I pray for the peace and welfare of the prison. May you bless and keep this prison and make Your face to shine upon it and be gracious to all who reside here. Lord, turn Your face to this prison and fill it with peace. May the peace of Christ rule in the hearts of all those who work here. And may I make every effort to keep the unity of the Spirit through the bond of peace. For You keep in perfect peace those whose minds are fixed on You because they trust in You. Thank You, Lord, for as I pray for the peace of the prison and for it to prosper, then so, too, will I prosper. In Jesus' name, Amen.

Family of Inmate Petition

Lord, I thank You that Your Word directs me and teaches me what to do. Today, I lift up in prayer (name of prison) where (name of person praying for) is exiled. I pray for the peace and welfare of the prison. May you bless and keep this prison and make Your face to shine upon it and be gracious to all who reside here. Lord, turn Your face to this prison and fill it with peace. May the peace of Christ rule in the hearts of all those who work there. And may (name of person praying for) make every effort to keep the unity of the Spirit through the bond of peace. For You keep in perfect peace those whose minds are fixed on You because they trust in You. Thank You, Lord, for as I pray for the peace of the prison, and for it to prosper, then so, too, shall (name of person praying for) prosper. In Jesus' name, Amen.

Prison Ministries

Prepare Yourself

Be sure you have prayed through the Preparing to Petition the Courtroom of Heaven prayers in chapter ten.

Preparing Your Case

Look up and meditate on these Scripture references: Hebrews 13:3; Matthew 9:38; Mark 16:15-18; Ephesians 3:16; 2 Timothy 2:15; Titus 2:11-15

Add any additional Scriptures the Lord shows you.

Inmate Petition

> Lord, I thank You for Your ministers who remember those who are in prison as if they themselves were also in prison. I ask You, the Lord of the harvest, to send Your chosen laborers to preach the good news and deliverance to the captives in this prison. I pray for ministers who fulfill the Great Commission of preaching the gospel to all people, including those of us inside these concrete walls, so that whoever believes will be saved. I pray that miraculous signs will follow those who believe so that demons will be cast out, they will speak in new languages, they will not be hurt if they pick up snakes or drink something deadly, and they will lay hands on the sick and see them get well.
>
> I ask You to give these ministers power through the Spirit to be strong and reinforced with mighty power

in their inner being. I pray that You pour out Your Spirit upon Your ministers and upon those who hear the message of hope spoken through their mouths.

I pray that Your ministers diligently study Your Word so they show themselves approved unto You as workmen who do not need to be put to shame, rightly dividing Your Word of truth.

Thank You, Lord, that the grace of God that saved me, also teaches me to turn from a godless lifestyle and turn to living a godly life as I wait for my glorious Savior to appear. In Jesus' name, Amen.

Family of Inmate Petition

Lord, I thank You for Your ministers who remember those who are in prison as if they themselves were also in prison. I ask You, the Lord of the harvest, to send Your chosen laborers to preach the good news and deliverance to the captives in (name of prison). I pray for ministers who will fulfill the Great Commission of preaching the gospel to all people, including those inside (name of prison) so that whoever believes will be saved. I pray that miraculous signs follow those who believe so that demons will be cast out, they will speak in new languages, they will not be hurt if they pick up snakes or drink something deadly, and they will lay hands on the sick and see them get well.

I ask You, Lord, to give these ministers power through the Spirit to be strong and reinforced with mighty power in their inner being. I pray that You pour out Your Spirit upon Your ministers and upon those who hear the message of hope spoken through their mouths. I pray that Your ministers diligently study Your Word so they show themselves approved unto You, workmen who do not need to be put to shame, rightly dividing Your Word of truth.

Thank You, Lord, that the grace of God that saved _____, also teaches him/her to turn from a godless lifestyle and turn to living a godly life as we wait for our glorious Savior to appear. In Jesus' name, Amen.

Comfort and Restoration for Victims

Prepare Yourself

Be sure you have prayed through the Preparing to Petition the Courtroom of Heaven prayers in chapter ten.

Prepare Your Case

Look up and meditate on these Scripture references: Exodus 15:2; Psalm 23:4; Isaiah 1:18; Colossians 3:13; Romans 15:13; Philippians 4:19; Romans 8:28; Isaiah 43:19; Joel 2:25; 2 Corinthians 5:17-19; Exodus 15:2

Add any additional Scriptures the Lord shows you.

Inmate Prayer for Victim(s) and Their Family

You, O Lord, are my strength and my song. You are my salvation. I will praise You and exalt You. I pray for _____ (name the victim(s) and their family) as they walk through the valley of the shadow of death. I pray that they will not fear any evil, because You are with them. May Your rod and staff comfort them. I pray You fill the victim(s) and their family with hope so they may abound in joy and peace by the power of the Holy Spirit. I ask You to supply all of their needs—physical, mental, and emotional healing, as well as finances—according to Your glorious riches in Christ Jesus. I pray that You take all the bad things that happened and make something good come out of it as You promise to work together all things for good for those who love You, those who are called according to Your purpose. You make pathways in the wilderness and create rivers in the barren lands. I ask You to restore to the victim(s) the years that the swarming locusts have eaten. The Enemy comes to steal, kill, and destroy, but Jesus came to give abundant life. I ask You to fill them with the abundant life that Jesus has for them.

Lord, I repent for the sins and offenses I have committed against the victim(s) and their family. And though my sins are like scarlet, You make them as white as snow. And though they are red like crimson, You make them as white as wool. In Christ, I am a new person. The old person who did those wrongs no longer exists. My new life in Christ has begun. You, my God, have reconciled me to Yourself in Christ, no longer holding my sins against me. I pray, Father, that as You heal the victim(s) and their family, they will release me through forgiveness so they may receive the fullness of Your healing and Your peace that surpasses all understanding. In Jesus' name, Amen.

Family of Inmate Prayer for Victim(s) and Their Family

You, O Lord, are my strength and my song. You are my salvation. I will praise You and exalt You. I pray for _____ (name the victim(s) and their family) as they walk through the valley of the shadow of death. I pray that they will not fear any evil, for You are with them. May Your rod and staff comfort them. I pray You fill the victim(s) and their family with hope so they may abound in joy and peace by the power of the Holy

Spirit. I ask You to supply all of their needs—physical, mental, and emotional healing, as well as finances—according to Your glorious riches in Christ Jesus. I pray that You take all the bad things that happened and make something good come out of it as You promise to work together all things for good for those who love You, those who are called according to Your purpose. You make pathways in the wilderness and create rivers in the barren lands. I ask You to restore to the victim(s) the years that the swarming locusts have eaten. The Enemy comes to steal, kill, and destroy, but Jesus came to give abundant life. I ask You to fill them with the abundant life that Jesus has for them.

Lord, thank You that the blood of Jesus paid the debt in full that _____ owed for the sins committed against the victim(s) and their family. And though these sins were like scarlet, You make them as white as snow. And though they were red like crimson, You make them as white as wool. In Christ, _____ is a new person. The old person who did those wrongs no longer exists. _____'s new life in Christ has begun. You have reconciled _____ to Yourself in Christ and no longer hold these sins against _____. I pray that as You heal the victims and their family, that they will release _____ to You through forgiveness so they may receive the fullness of Your healing and Your peace that surpasses all understanding. In Jesus' name, Amen.

Praise to Our God

The prayer of praise is the purest form of prayer, because we focus entirely on God. When we magnify Him and who He is, the cares of this world that consume us begin to shrink. Praise brings us into His presence, for God inhabits the praises of His people (see Psalm 22:3).

Praise communicates our desire to show God our appreciation, thankfulness, love, devotion, and reverence toward Him. When we offer up the prayer of praise, it changes our heart, mind, and attitude. Please note, none of this happens in an instant. When we make praise a daily part of our life, we will see a difference day by day. It is just like planting a seed in the ground. It must be watered and nurtured before you see the plant grow.

I've put together the following prayer of praise to get you started. I encourage you to look up praise Scriptures and put together your own prayers of praise to the Lord. I also encourage you to begin and conclude your prayer time with praise to the Father for the mercies you have received in the courtroom of heaven and for granting the petitions you've requested. Even if you do not see the answers yet, when petitions are based on the Word of God, you can be confident the answers are on their way. We leave the how and the when up to God, the Righteous Judge.

Give Praise to God

Lord, You made this day, and I will rejoice and be glad in it. When I call upon You, the One who is worthy to be praised, You save me from my enemies. I will give thanks and sing praises to Your name. I will sing and celebrate and praise Your power. I will sing praises as I remember all You have done.

Lord, You have turned my mourning into dancing. You have taken my sorrow and filled me with joy. I will not be silent but will give You thanks forever. I will continually bless you, Lord, and proclaim Your greatness.

My soul shall boast in You, Lord. The humble will hear of it and be glad. Come and magnify the Lord with me. Let us exalt His holy name together. I will sing praises for You are my defense, my God of mercy. Praise the Lord! I give thanks for You are good and Your mercy, lovingkindness, and faithful love endures forever. Through Christ, I continually offer up the sacrifice of praise to God, the fruit of my lips giving thanks to Your name. Praise God! Hallelujah! For the Omnipotent Lord God reigns!

Scripture References: Psalm 118:24; Psalm 18:3; Psalm 18:49; Psalm 21:13; Psalm 30:4; Psalm 30:11-12; Psalm 34:1-3; Psalm 48:1; Psalm 59:17; Psalm 106:1; Hebrews 13:15; Revelation 19:5-6

Conclusion

Your Work Will Be Rewarded

Prayer does not equip us for greater works—
prayer is the greater work.

~ Oswald Chambers

When my son was arrested and later convicted, I had absolutely no control over the circumstances. There was nothing I could do to fix it, undo it, or press rewind on time. What was done was done.

I'm a fixer by nature. When my kids were little and came to me with a boo-boo, I kissed it to make it better. If my husband asked for something, I did everything I could to make it happen for him.

I prefer to have a plan of action for life's situations, implement the plan, then see the desired result. That's called *control*. Being a fixer is being a controller. I have had to go through the school of hard knocks to realize that controlling my circumstances was merely an illusion. The only thing I have control over is my response to a situation.

Now, with my son locked behind concrete walls and barbed wire fences, I can't fix it.

Am I without hope? Absolutely not. And neither are you.

Thank God, we have a place to go. We make our appeals to the courtroom of heaven and lift our petitions to the highest court—the throne room of grace and mercy in the kingdom of God.

In my despair after my son's conviction, I didn't know what else to do, so I prayed Psalm 17:6: *I am praying to you because I know you will answer, O God. Bend down and listen as I pray* (NLT). I pleaded with God to change our circumstances, for I felt they were more than I could bear.

When grief struck me, it hit with a deadly blow that started the internal spiritual bleeding. Yet prayer and the hope I had in God's Word sustained me.

Yes, prayer is work. But God promises our work will be rewarded. One day while reading Scriptures, the following words from Jeremiah 31:16-17 (NKJV) resonated in my spirit;

> Thus says the LORD:
> "Refrain your voice from weeping,
> And your eyes from tears;
> For your work shall be rewarded," says the Lord.
> "And they shall come back from the land of the enemy.
> There is hope in your future," says the Lord,
> "That your children shall come back to their own border."

The Lord impressed on my heart that my work—the appeals I make to the courtroom of heaven through my prayers—shall be rewarded. I continue to hold on to the promise and look forward to the day my son will return home. Not as the *old man* he was before prison, but as a new creation in Christ as the Lord prepares him for his greater purpose in life.

So far, the rewards I have received from the prayer work are peace and joy from the Lord. The kind of peace that does not rely on circumstances, but on my relationship with the Father through Jesus Christ my Lord. My faith is growing. My trust in God is increasing. Day by day, the broken places in my heart continue to heal as I surrender to Him, walking through repentance and forgiveness. I no longer suffer from the anxiety and depression that placed me in my own personal prison, keeping me from participating in life. Many of the prayers found in this book have been answered for me personally. That is a great reward from the courtroom of heaven.

Continue the work of repentance. Walk in forgiveness daily. And petition the Lord in the courtroom of heaven according to His Word. You, too, will experience His rewards!

A Final Note from the Author

My family and I traveled through a horrific ordeal. My emotional healing from this calamity transpired over many years. It did not happen in a day, a few weeks, or several months. The testimony of the hope I have in the Lord came as I consistently sought Him day by day in His Word and through prayer. God's gifts of repentance and forgiveness through Jesus Christ led to the healing of my broken heart.

As painful as it was for us to navigate through the days that followed that tragic night, the repercussions this tragedy caused the victims' families can never be undone.

My family and I pray for those affected by my son's role that tragic night. I am so sorry, and I wish this had never happened. But I am powerless to change the past.

My prayers are the best I have to offer the families. We thank God the young woman survived the severe stabbing. In her father's victim impact statement, he testified his daughter may never walk without assistance. Since we do not know the status of her rehabilitation, we continue to pray for her miraculous and complete recovery. For both families, we pray for their total healing and restoration that only comes through Jesus.

As for the main perpetrator of the crimes that night, he accepted a forty-eight-year sentence from the state. We pray he meets Jesus, repents, and serves the Lord during his confinement.

By sharing my story from a mother's perspective, I pray it encourages those who have lost hope in the midst of despair. Because the Lord turns the worst situations around for His glory, we all have hope for the future when we humble ourselves and appeal to the courtroom of heaven.

Recommended Resources

For further courtroom of heaven prayer study:

From the Courtroom of Heaven to the Throne of Grace and Mercy, Jeanette Strauss (Glorious Creations, 2011)

From the Courtroom of Heaven: Prayers and Petitions, Jeanette Strauss (Glorious Creations, 2013)

Operating in the Courts of Heaven: Granting God the Legal Right to Fulfill His Passion and Answer Our Prayers, Robert Henderson, (Global Reformers, 2016)

Prayers & Declarations That Open the Courts of Heaven, Robert Henderson, (Destiny Image, 2018)

Silencing the Accuser-Third Edition: Restoration of Your Birthright, Jacquelin Hanselman (God's Foundation Builders, 2016)

For understanding the enemy's tactics and freedom in Jesus:

Shadow Boxing: The Dynamic 2-5-14 Strategy to Defeat the Darkness Within, Dr. Henry Malone (Vision Life Publications,

Healing the Wounded Soul: Break Free from the Pain of the Past and Live Again, Katie Souza (Charisma House, 2017)

Free book and discipleship newsletter for prisoners

Send your request for the book *Jail-House Religion* and ask to be added to the Discipleship Newsletter mailing list by writing to:

Freedom in Jesus Ministries
Attn: Stephen – JHR/SW
P.O. Box 939
Levelland, TX 79336

Support for families of prisoners

Fortress of Hope Ministries
P.O. Box 65763
Lubbock, TX 79464

FortressofHopeMinistries.com

ENDNOTES

CHAPTER 1

1 "Arrest." Dictionary.com. Accessed July 11, 2019. http:// www.dictionary.com/browse/arrest?s=t

2 Donald Miller, "You Are Who Your Friends Are." Relevant. Last modified May 12, 2010. https://relevantmagazine. com/life5/relationships/you-are-who-your-friends-are/

CHAPTER 2

1 Canfield, Jack, Mark Victor Hansen, and Tom Lagana. *Chicken Soup for the Prisoner's Soul: 101 Stories to Open the Heart and Rekindle the Spirit of Hope, Healing and Forgiveness*. Cos Cob, CT: Backlist LLC, 2012, p. 128

CHAPTER 3

1 "Publications." Publications. Accessed October 17, 2017. https://www.americanbar.org/groups/criminal_justice/ publications/.

2 Study.com. Accessed October 23, 2017. http://study.com/ articles/District_Attorney_Career_Info_and_Education_ Requirements.html.

3 "Grand Jury Proceedings." Texas Grand Jury. Accessed October 23, 2017. http://www.wilderdwidefense.com/ criminal-defense/texas-grand-jury-proceedings

4 "Information & Indictment in Texas." General Law. Accessed October 23, 2017. https://texasdefenselaw.com/ library/information-indictment-texas/

5   "Pretrial Process." Criminal Law. Accessed October 23, 2017   http://www.bobbydalebarina.com/criminal-law/how-does-the-pretrial-process-work-in-texas/

6   "Pretrial Process." Texas Defense Law. Accessed October 23, 2017. https://texasdefenselaw.com/library/texas-pre-trial-process/

7   Strong, J. (2009). *A Concise Dictionary of the Words in the Greek Testament and The Hebrew Bible* (Vol. 1, p. 41). Bellingham, WA: Logos Bible Software.

8   Stählin, G. (1964–). αἰτέω, αἴτημα, ἀπαιτέω, ἐξαιτέω, παραιτέομαι. G. Kittel, G. W. Bromiley, & G. Friedrich (Eds.), *Theological Dictionary of the New Testament* (electronic ed., Vol. 1, p. 194). Grand Rapids, MI: Eerdmans.

9   Strongs NT 476 THAYER'S GREEK LEXICON, Electronic Database. Copyright © 2002, 2003, 2006, 2011 by Biblesoft, Inc. All rights reserved. Used by permission. BibleSoft.com

10   Strauss, Jeanette, *From the Courtroom of Heaven: Prayers and Petitions*, Quincy, MI, Glorious Creations, 2013, pp. 20-21

CHAPTER 4
1   Jonathan R. Tung, Esq. "Can a Felon Become a Lawyer?" *FindLaw* (blog). Accessed October 14, 2017. http://blogs.findlaw.com/greedy_associates/2015/12/can-a-felon-become-a-lawyer.html

CHAPTER 5
1   "What is a Judge's Role in Court?" FindLaw. Accessed April 27, 2017. http://litigation.findlaw.com/legal-system/what-is-a-judges-role-in-court.html

2   "Exclusionary Rule." Legal Dictionary. Last modified November 17, 2014. https://legaldictionary.net/exclusionary-rule/

3   Jessica Tran. "What is Admissible Evidence?" Legal Match. Last modified April 11, 2018. http://www.legalmatch.com/law-library/article/what-is-admissible-evidence.html

4   "Role of the Judge and Other Courtroom Participants." United States District Court Northern District of Florida. Accessed October 27, 2017. http://www.flnd.uscourts.gov/role-judge-and-other-courtroom-participants

CHAPTER 6

1   "Penal Code: Title 2. General Principles of Criminal Responsibilities." Texas Statutes. Accessed October 27, 2017. http://www.statutes.legis.state.tx.us/Docs/PE/htm/PE.7.htm

2   Bevere, John, *Driven by Eternity: 10th Anniversary Edition*, Palmer Lake, CO, Messenger International, Inc., 2016, p. 12

3   Pat Robertson. "What is the Great White Throne Judgment?" CBN. Accessed October 27, 2017. https://www1.cbn.com/questions/great-white-throne-judgment

4   "The Great White Throne Judgment – What is it?" Compelling Truth. Accessed October 27, 2017. https://www.compellingtruth.org/great-white-throne-judgment.html

5   Charles Stanley, Dr. "Your Convictions About the Judgment of the Believer." In Touch. Accessed October 27, 2017. https://www.intouch.org/-/media/sermon-notes/your-convictions-about-the-judgment-of-the-believer.ashx

6   Blackaby, Henry T., King, Claude V., *Fresh Encounter: God's Pattern for Revival and Spiritual Awakening*, Nashville, TN, Lifeway Press, 1993, p. 62-65

CHAPTER 8

1   Emily Green. "What is the First Step Act?" Prison Fellowship. Accessed February 6, 2019. https://www.prisonfellowship.org/2019/01/what-is-the-first-step-act/

2   Whitaker, Kent, *Murder by Family: The Incredible True Story of a Son's Treachery and a Father's Forgiveness*, New York, NY, Howard Books, 2008, pp. 12-13

3   McGuire, Gene, *Unshackled: From Ruin to Redemption*, Tulsa, OK, Emerge Publishing, 2017, p. 219

4   Robert Hull, "Katie Souza: God's Love Found in Lockdown." Accessed May 11, 2018. http://www1.cbn.com/700club/katie-souza-gods-love-found-lockdown

5   Joe Narvais, "Any Day Now," Gospel Tract Society, Inc., Independence, MO

CHAPTER 9

1   Strauss, Jeanette, *From the Courtroom of Heaven to the Throne of Grace and Mercy* Quincy, MI, Glorious Creations, 2011, p. 20

2   Arndt, W., Danker, F. W., Bauer, W., & Gingrich, F. W. (2000). *A Greek-English lexicon of the New Testament and other early Christian literature* (3rd ed., p. 985). Chicago: University of Chicago Press.

3   Malone, Henry, *Shadowboxing: The Dynamic 2-5-14 Strategy to Defeat the Darkness Within*, Lewisville, TX, Vision Life Publications, 2011, p. 89

CHAPTER 10

1   Strauss, Jeanette, *From the Courtroom of Heaven: Prayers & Petitions to the Throne of Grace and Mercy* Quincy, MI, Glorious Creations, 2013, p. 25

PETITIONS FOR THE COURTROOM OF HEAVEN

1 Psalm 118:28 NLT
2 Psalm 118:28 NLT
3 Psalm 103:1-5 NLT
4 Psalm 103:1-2 NLT
5 Jeremiah 10:6-7 NLT
6 1 Corinthians 13:4-7 NLT
7 Jeremiah 10:6-7 NLT
8 1 Corinthians 13:4-7 NLT
9 Psalm 43:3-4 NLT
10 Psalm 43:3-4 NLT
11 Psalm 68:4 NLT
12 Psalm 68:4 NLT
13 Psalm 5:11 NLT
14 Psalm 5:11 NLT
15 Psalm 9:1-2 NLT
16 Psalm 9:1-2 NLT
17 Psalm 118:28 NLT
18 Psalm 118:28 NLT
19 Psalm 103:1-5 NLT

PLEAD YOUR CASE IN THE COURTROOM OF HEAVEN!

Ask your family and friends to purchase a copy
to pray effectively for one another.